> Salam Pax

Salam Pax is a pseudonym. He lives in Baghdad, Iraq.

'"Salam Pax" is an extremely talented writer. The singularity of his position and subject matter can lead one to overlook this, but I was aware of it as soon as I started reading him, just prior to the war. The fact that English is not his first language actually underscores his gifts of observation and expression; he'll write "around" his own uncertainty of usage, and get it right on the button.' **William Gibson**

'The most vivid account of the Iraq conflict' **Guardian**

'Salam Pax not only highlighted the deficiencies of embedded media, [his] blog became required reading for anyone needing to find out what was really happening on the ground during the US-led invasion.' **Globe and Mail**

'The reliable chronicler of the chaos' **Spiegel**

'A mysterious Iraqi who goes by the name of "Salam Pax" and who writes a blog (internet diary) from Baghdad is becoming a celebrity, on the internet, with his first-hand stories of a city under siege . . . the traffic on the site has become so intense that it has blocked the server, while his e-mail has gone on the blink due to the vast number of messages from people who are asking him to prove his true identity.' **La Stampa**

'Salam Pax, the anonymous Iraqi blogger who went worryingly silent during the US invasion, is back. And he makes up by clearing the backlog . . . His account of Baghdad since the liberation is fascinating. It is far better than anything you'll read in the newspapers. Things you wouldn't have known: Thuraya satphones are the ultimate Baghdad status symbol; there's utter contempt for the exiles who've appropriated the best real estate (Chalabi's group took over Salam's sports club); locals would shoo out the Syrian Fedayeen creeps for fear they'd attract American retaliation; and Salam likes the communists, who are at least honest. It's great stuff.' **Nick Denton**

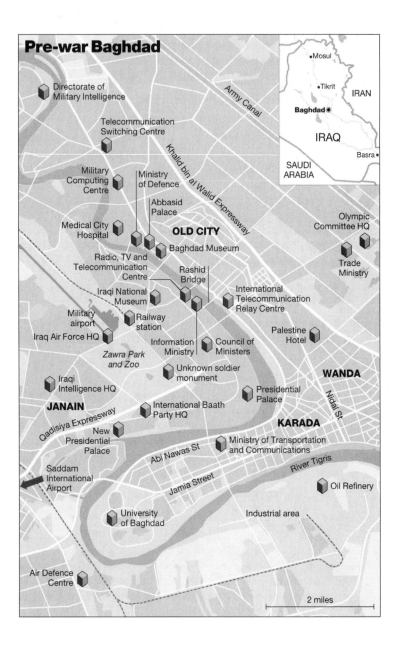

Pre-war Baghdad

Directorate of Military Intelligence

Telecommunication Switching Centre

Military Computing Centre

Ministry of Defence

Abbasid Palace

Medical City Hospital

OLD CITY

Baghdad Museum

Radio, TV and Telecommunication Centre

Rashid Bridge

Iraqi National Museum

International Telecommunication Relay Centre

Military airport

Railway station

Iraq Air Force HQ

Zawra Park and Zoo

Information Ministry

Council of Ministers

Palestine Hotel

Iraqi Intelligence HQ

Unknown soldier monument

WANDA

JANAIN

International Baath Party HQ

Presidential Palace

Nidal St

Qadisiya Expressway

New Presidential Palace

KARADA

Ministry of Transportation and Communications

Abi Nawas St

Saddam International Airport

Jamia Street

River Tigris

Oil Refinery

University of Baghdad

Industrial area

Air Defence Centre

2 miles

Khalid bin al Walid Expressway

Army Canal

Olympic Committee HQ

Trade Ministry

•Mosul

•Tikrit

IRAN

Baghdad◉

IRAQ

Basra •

SAUDI ARABIA

> Salam Pax
THE CLANDESTINE DIARY OF AN ORDINARY IRAQI

Salam Pax

GROVE PRESS
New York

First published in Great Britain in 2003 by Atlantic Books, on behalf of Guardian
Newspapers Ltd., London, England

The author and publisher would like to thank all the bloggers who have contributed
to this book.

Printed in the United States of America
Published simultaneously in Canada

FIRST AMERICAN EDITION

Library of Congress Cataloging-in-Publication Data on file at the Library of Congress

ISBN 0-8021-4044-0

Design by Richard Marston
Map of Pre-war Baghdad, p. ii, by Finbarr Sheehy

Grove Press
841 Broadway
New York, NY 10003

03 04 05 06 07   10 9 8 7 6 5 4 3 2 1

The West won the world not by the superiority of its ideas or values or religion but rather by its superiority in applying organized violence. Westerners often forget this fact, non-Westerners never do.

Samuel P. Huntington

Contents

Introduction

I came relatively late to 'Where is Raed?',[+] the enigmatically named web-site on which most of the material in this book first appeared. A week or so before the bombs began falling (I mean the last lot, as Salam might say), a colleague had e-mailed me about a remarkable web diary apparently being written by a savvy young Iraqi man somewhere in suburban Baghdad. By then Salam Pax was a firm favourite with the international community of bloggers – the swelling band of electronic motor mouths whose self-published diatribes, musings and banalities have become the Internet's most compelling new phenomenon. His own weblog was being linked to by more sites than any other and the web bristled with debate about his true identity. Within a minute or two of entering the Baghdad Blogger's quirky, acutely observed world, I could see why.

Salam's diary was quite simply the freshest, most exciting writing coming out of Iraq. Two things about it were instantly striking. The first was its almost giddy irreverence about Saddam's regime. Whereas foreign journalists needed the Baathist equivalent of a PhD in kremlinology to parse the ritualistic declarations of fealty by ordinary Iraqis for any indication of dissent, Salam treated his rulers with (very) thinly veiled contempt.

The second was that he was just like us. By now we had got used to a portrayal of Iraqis as poor, anti-Western, frequently hysterical and altogether very different from us; here was one who addressed us in perfect idiomatic English, was obsessed with David Bowie lyrics and awaited the release of the new Massive Attack album as eagerly as any Glastonbury regular. One of my favourite entries in

---

[+] dear_raed.blogspot.com.

the blog described a defiant visit to a Baghdad music store days before the start of the war, after which he reported with some satisfaction that The Deftones and the Black Rebel Motorcycle Club had 'joined the Pax Radio CD racks'.

Another ingredient added to the diary's powerful, subversive appeal: it was, heaven forfend, very funny. Salam appeared to delight in recording in actuarial detail the blackest absurdities of his – and his country's – predicament. On 11 February he broke from a reflection on George Bush's style of diplomacy to report that DJs on Baghdad's English-language radio station were not allowed to refer to the band Bush by name. 'They have to spell it: "Bee yu ess etch have yet another single out." I bet all the DJs there thank God there isn't a band called Schwartzkopf.' A few weeks later, he was ruthlessly lampooning a BBC reporter for referring to Iraqis maintaining an air of normality. 'Look, what are you supposed to do? Run around in the streets wailing? War is at the door eeeeeeeeeeeee!' He ended that entry with a list of 'other normal stuff we did this week'. It included taping up his home windows, installing a manual water pump and buying face-masks.

Under the circumstances it wasn't surprising that some people thought the Baghdad Blogger was too good to be true. Salam's appetite for verbal tricksiness – his pseudonym is a play on the word 'peace' in Arabic and Latin, while the address of the site contains the palindrome 'dearraed' – only fuelled the speculation. Wonderfully, the conviction of those who believed that he was a Baathist agent was matched only by the suspicion of others that he was a Mossad or CIA operative. Some web commentators conducted elaborate technical checks on his e-mails to establish where he was posting from; others cited their own contacts with him as evidence of his bona fides. I was never in any doubt: Salam's diaries were simply too detailed, too accurate and too insightful – they *smelled* of the place – to be anything other than the real thing.

Salam had begun his blog six months earlier as a way of keeping in touch with his friend, Raed, who had moved to study in Jordan. Now he seemed genuinely nonplussed by the fuss it was creating. When I e-mailed him asking permission to run extracts from it in the *Guardian* he replied: '*shrug* It is getting out of control and blown beyond what it is and getting far too much attention. Do what you like. But everybody is making a huge deal out of it.' On 24 March, two days after the onslaught on Baghdad began, we published an electrifying extract describing the build-up to war in the Iraqi capital. It ended: '6.05 p.m. Two more hours until the B52s get to Iraq.'

For four days, Salam did not update his site – and then, on 25 March, a terse account of the first few days of the conflict appeared. The usual brio was conspicuously absent. 'People (and I bet "allied forces") were expecting things to be much easier,' he wrote. 'There are no waving masses of people welcoming the Americans, nor are they surrendering by the thousands. People are doing what all of us are: sitting in their homes hoping that a bomb doesn't fall on them and keeping their doors shut.'

Agonisingly, he did not post again for the duration of the conflict. The e-mails I sent every few days went unanswered. I wrote to Diana Moon, the wonderful New York blogger who had become Salam's closest net friend and asked her to forward my messages. Still nothing. We hoped for the best (that he had lost access to the Internet) and feared the worst (discovery by Saddam's Mukhabarat? A wayward coalition bomb?).

Then on 7 May, a month after Saddam's statue was wrenched from its pedestal in Al-Firdaws Square, the e-mail grapevine began to buzz: Salam had posted again, with a little help from Diana Moon. Though he had lost his net access, he had not lost the blogging habit. Throughout the war he kept a notebook diary, meticulously recording the war as viewed from Hotel Pax, the name he gave his suburban home after numerous relatives took refuge there. Salam's wartime postings seesawed between the camp jauntiness of his earlier diaries and a bleaker voice than anything we had encountered yet.

On 25 March he wrote: 'In the oh-the-irony-of-it-all section of my life I can add the unbelievable bad luck that when I wanted to watch a movie, because I got sick of all the news, the only movie I had which I have not seen a hundred times is *The American President*. No joke. A friend gave me that video months ago and I never watched it. I did last night. The American "presidential palace" looks quite good. But Michael Douglas is a sad ass president.' He also found time to complain about his hayfever. But by

2 April, all he could muster was this: 'Actually too tired, scared and burnt-out to write anything. Yes, we did go out again to see what was hit. Yes, everything just hurts . . . I can't stand the TV or the lies on the news any more. No good news wherever you look.'

Aside from confirmation that he was alive and well, Salam's 7 May post offered a tantalising clue to his identity. In passing he mentioned that his close friend G., a regular fixture in the blog, had done some translation work for the *Guardian* in Baghdad. We immediately mailed all the *Guardian* correspondents who had reported from the Iraqi capital asking if they could identify G. Two of them could and within a week or so, a meeting had been set up with Salam himself. The interview he eventually gave to Rory McCarthy filled in many of the blanks that had preoccupied his legion of fans.

We learned that his command of Western culture – if not his elegant English – was the product of two lengthy spells living in Vienna, one of them while studying for a degree in architecture. We learned that he posted either from the offices of the architecture firm where he worked or from a CD-strewn bedroom decorated with a poster for *The Matrix*. His own father, he told McCarthy, had not known about his illicit chronicle until hearing an item about the Baghdad Blogger on the BBC World Service and confronting his son. And more than once, he feared Saddam's secret policemen had finally caught up with him: 'I spent a couple of days thinking this is the end. And then you wait for a couple of days and nothing happens and you say, "OK, let's do it again." Stupid risks, one after another.'

Since there were still plenty of people in Baghdad who might take exception to his candour, the one piece of the puzzle that Salam asked us to withhold was his real surname (Salam is his real first name). But elsewhere, others were making their own deductions. The *New York Times* reporter Peter Maass wrote memorably about the moment he realized the Baghdad Blogger had been right under his nose. 'I laughed out loud . . . I howled. Salam Pax, the most famous and most mysterious blogger in the world, was my interpreter.'

Unusually for an Internet phenomenon, Salam successfully made the transition into old media with a fortnightly column in the

Guardian, two of which reappear in this book. The columns, whether railing about the political inertia of Iraqi students or contrasting the styles of British and American soldiers, have exhibited the same telling eye for detail and dry wit that made his blog a must-read. In one of his first columns he reflected on the profusion of newspapers springing up in the city. 'There are two questions which no one can answer: how many political parties are there now in Iraq? And how many newspapers are printed weekly . . . I am thinking of getting my own: *Pax News – All the Rumours, All the Time.*'

By the end of the war Salam's celebrity had spread far beyond the Internet. There were Salam Pax T-shirts and mugs. Nick Denton called him the 'Anne Frank of the war' and Peter Maass added 'and its Elvis'. But his increasingly high profile attracted a new, less welcome form of attention too. Those who thought his blog was unduly critical of Iraq's 'liberators' made dark insinuations about his parents' Baathist connections. Eventually Salam blew his top, advising his detractors to 'go play Agatha Christie somewhere else.' His mother, he said, had been a sociologist at the Ministry of Education, but had given up her job when she was told she could not make progress in her career without becoming a Party member. His father had been an eminent economist, but had made a similar decision when faced with the same choice. 'You are being disrespectful to the people who have put the first copy of George Orwell's *Nineteen Eighty-Four* in my hands . . . go fling the rubbish at someone else.'

In fact, the conspiracy theorists' preoccupation with his family's supposed regime connections misses one of the most compelling attributes of Salam's diaries: he directs his vitriol in *all* directions. In the last days of the war he managed to describe the Fedayeen, the Baathist loyalists mounting a guerilla defence of Baghdad in the space of two paragraphs as 'sickos', 'chicken shit' and 'creepy fucks'. If he has been less than reverential about Iraq's occupiers, he has been harder still on their Iraqi critics. And like a wild animal reminding us he has no intention of being tamed, he has not allowed his mainstream success to dent the blogger's instinctive suspicion of us old media types. After his interview with McCarthy, he wrote in his blog: 'I sold my soul to the devil. I talked to Rory from the *Guardian*. Look, he paid for a great lunch in a place which had air-conditioning and lots of people from Foreign. It was fun talking to him, but when Raed saw me after "the talk" he said I looked like someone had violated me. So there is a bit of guilt. But that was washed away with the cool air-conditioning. Yeah, I am cheap like that. I would sell my parents for a nice bottle of wine.'

Ian Katz
Guardian Features Editor

> Salam Pax

Saturday, 7 September 2002

I'm preparing my emergency lists these days – any suggestions are welcome. At the moment I have:

Candles

Alcohol (maybe red wine?)

Good books

Crunchy munchies.

I think that will get me thru the bombing quite nicely.

:: **salam pax 12:52 PM [+]** ::

Thursday, 19 September 2002

I hate birthdays.

But I'm not going to whine about why this year was the worst ever (I had the best days of my life for five or six months at the beginning of this year and it has been a constant downhill after that).

I give you five thoughts which gave me the warm fuzzies:

1. Linkylove from the Legendary Monkey:✛ she digs Portishead and has magnetic poetry. I have fallen in love with her fridge. Now I'm practising my low-frequency hums, to get those communication issues out of the way.

✛ Host of the Sudden Nothing website: vaspider.surreally.net/suddennothing.

2. Raed calling me at midnight and telling me this is the last year I will be able to say 'I'm in my twenties.' Not funny. He thinks it is and laughed and laughed. Cruel bastard.

3. Friends and relatives finally realizing that I'm not good at these things and usually show my grumpy bitch side on these days. So instead of crashing my gates, I got e-mails and phone calls full of good wishes and love (but none wishing me what I really needed: seeing him and knowing that he is safe and well).

4. Watching *Dancer in the Dark* again. I ♥ Björk.

:: salam pax 12:05 PM [+] ::

I really wish Massive Attack would start worrying about the delay in their album release rather than this.** But it is good to know that these people care about what is happening in Iraq and I was really very excited about the news that Massive Attack are planning a demonstration and a petition-signing with CND. The forum is great. The regulars there have a very quirky sense of humour.

Did you know that Massive Attack changed their name in 1991 to Massive only because the release of *Blue Lines* was too close to, ahem, the 'Mother of all Battles'. Now you know.

Today at work I was told that I am not getting paid this month. 'Cashflow trouble' da boss said. For some reason I thought that was funny. I couldn't control my giggles. He thought I am having a nervous breakdown or something. Short of telling you 'You're fired' this is the funniest thing evil-boss-creature could tell you on your birthday.

:: salam pax 1:01 PM [+] ::

Saturday, 21 September 2002

All fools who spend their weekend working, although they have

----
✦ Host of the Sudden Nothing website: vaspider.surreally.net/suddennothing.

✦✦ 'No Massive Attack!', an article in the *New Musical Express*: www.nme.com/news/102988.htm. Damon Albarn (of the pop group Blur) and Robert '3-D' Del Naja (of Massive Attack) delivered an open letter outlining their opposition to an invasion of Iraq to Tony Blair, the British Prime Minister, on 18 September 2002.

been told they are not getting paid, please stand on this side of the line.

I really had nothing better to do. Besides, I forgot how much I like working with the VIZ⁺ software. (I didn't get a chance to show you the work I did for the 100 Bed Hospital when I was in Jordan. I'll post the images here later.) I'm trying release four. It has a crazy right-click menu – I orgasm every time I click it. Do you see that red rectangular thingy in the image? *That* is the context menu for an editable mesh with a slice modifier. I love it.

Anyway, back to this world.

I checked my stats today and found out that I have been linked by Pandavox. That's the second link in two days. The goddess of linkylove has blessed me. Burning that modem and doing my sacred linkwhore dance around it worked. Go check Pandavox, you'll be surprised. I sit between Israeli and Iranian blogs – very geographically correct!

What really caught my eye was a post entitled 'A war to end wars'. I would really like to have some of that stuff you were on while writing this. Pandavox, honeybuns, you cannot be serious.

Iraq: First we take Baghdad.⁺⁺

Yeah . . . and then we take Berlin (Leonard Cohen has always been one of my favourite lyricists).

The Iraqi people will experience a prosperity unknown to them. The Iraqi people will see they have a friend with the American people. Most importantly, Iraq will no longer contribute money to terrorist groups.

Sure. We will contribute cheap reliable oil to keep western economies going. Awww Pandavox, how I wish things were as clear-cut as you put them in your little fairytale.

After their hostile governments collapse, many of the radical Islamists will lose a reason for fighting. Then we can enjoy peace again for a while.

⁺ An architectural modelling software by Kinetix.
⁺⁺ pandavox.blogspot.com.

Meg Ryan should be in this movie. She does this bad-turns-to-good-and-happy thing quite well.

It's 3 a.m. and I should go to sleep. Tomorrow we're having a meeting at the Ministry of Health and I have three Lebanese engineers from the consultancy to entertain.

Raed, if I put a commenting link would you use it?

:: **salam pax 3:45 AM [+]** ::

After three months of clear skies and fierce morning sun we have a cloudy morning with temperatures around 29°C/85°F. Mmmmmm, cool cloudy skies I love you.

Good article in *The Economist*: 'Whatever their quiet wish to be rid of Saddam Hussein, their experience of American arms has not been pleasant.'[+] And a funny cover for this week's print edition.

OK. Have to run now.

:: **salam pax 9:47 AM [+]** ::

Sunday, 22 September 2002

Got the OK for the comments link from Raed. I don't do nothing without Master Raed sayin' it's fine with him first. And here is another article in the *New York Times* about the war plans. I'm actually getting tired of these. Damn it, just do it and let us get over it!

> **Officials said, however, that any attack would begin with a lengthy air campaign led by B-2 bombers armed with 2,000-pound satellite-guided bombs to knock out Iraqi command and control headquarters and air defenses. They said a principal goal of the aerial bombardment would be to sever most communications from Baghdad and isolate Saddam Hussein from his commanders in the rest of the country.[++]**

:: **salam pax 3:00 AM [+]** ::

[+] From 'Saddam plays his ace' (19 September 2002) in *The Economist* (www.economist.com).

[++] 'Bush Has Received Pentagon Options on Attacking Iraq' (21 September 2002) by Eric Schmitt and David E. Sanger in the *New York Times* (www.nytimes.com).

Monday, 23 September 2002

The last couple of days I have been working in a double shift: 9 a.m. to 2 p.m. and come back at 5.30 or 6 p.m. and stay till 12 or so. I can't do the 3-D model thingy during the day, so I have to come back in the evening. I don't really mind. I like working with VIZ. Besides, being here with no one in the office I can crank up the volume and jump around while my sluggish computer renders the scenes.

Music for VIZ Modelling:
Toufic Farroukh: *Drab:zeen* (really good arabic/jazz/dance fusion)
Röyksopp: *Melody A.M.*
Timo Maas: *Loud* (and take a break when 'that's how I've been dancing' comes up to jump around)
David Bowie: *Heathen*
Lamb: *What Sound*

And remember: never ever try to do work or drive while listening to Björk or Aphex Twin – they do strange things to brain cells.

:: salam pax 7:26 PM [+] ::

Tuesday, 24 September 2002

Today I found out that WE HAVE PRESIDENTIAL ELECTIONS on the 15th of October. Well, I did know, but didn't know the date. I can't decide if I should laugh or cry, but it is more funny than tragic.

:: salam pax 9:56 AM [+] ::

Just read this in the *Guardian*:

> . . . like so many Iraqis after 20 years of war, [he is] a fatalist. He smokes heavily, *loves high-cholesterol foods* and is preparing his hospital for US attack.[+]

His love for 'high-cholesterol foods'??? What, is that another violation against UN sanctions? Let's make this clear, if people are

----
[+] 'After 20 years of war, Iraqi doctors await attack with mix of fatalism and dismay' (19 September 2002) by Ewan MacAskill in the *Guardian* (www.guardian.co.uk).

going to come here and demolish all high-cholesterol food produc-
tion plants I will not sit by and watch. Fight for your right to have a
heart attack! And just like me he also wants a bicycle:

> The general population has been getting ready too. 'Everyone has
> extra food, water, oil, candles, *bicycles*. You should have these
> things because of the threat,' he said . . .⁺

Suddenly Iraqis are turning to environmentally friendly transportation.

Very funny people those British, they really are.

Raed, are you really going to stay in Jordan and miss all the action?
Don't get married – come here and let's get bombed.

:: **salam pax 10:22 AM [+]** ::

Wednesday, 25 September 2002

Sorry honeybunny, no images today as I have exceeded my bandwidth limit.

Raed, since you are my rich friend abroad, why don't you pay for my
image-hosting account at villagephotos.com?

:: **salam pax 12:04 PM [+]** ::

Saturday, 28 September 2002

So what do you think is the most used word in our vocabulary
these days? It is 'ba3deen' (for you non-Arablish-speaking people,
it means 'later/afterwards'). Anything that has anything to do with
a decision that will affect the future will be answered with
'BA3DEEN'.

Example 1
[salam]: Listen . . . I haven't been paid the last two months and you
make me work like a slave. How about buying me a better mon-
itor than the one I have? It flickers.

⁺ See note on previous page.

[evil_boss_unit]: We will think about it 'ba3deen'.

[salam]: What 'afterwards'? After I have lost my eyesight?

[evil_boss_unit]: No. Who cares about you these days? Wait until after *it* happens.

[salam]: Whaaa? I don't . . . ohhh, you mean *it*. Oh, I guess it's OK then, we'll see what happens afterwards.

Example 2

[salam]: Awww GOD! You still have those hideous curtains! You promised they will not stay!

[female_parental_unit]: Oh . . . I thought I'll keep them and change them afterwards.

[salam]: They are ugly and there is no excuse for not changing them . . . you know that!!

[female_parental_unit]: I said 'ba3deen' . . . and if it makes you feel any better they will probably be shredded by all the glass that will be flying thru them.

[salam]: Oh you mean *that* . . . OK, wait till 'ba3deen'.

Raed is in Baghdad for a couple of days and since we have very clear skies at the moment and a beautiful half-moon is rising, Raed and Salam are taking their drinks to the roof and thinking about what to do 'ba3deen', under the half-moon sky.

And in the warm fuzzies department: Raed did offer to pay the subscription fee for my account (it pays having rich, reckless friends and NO I don't know what a leech is . . .), but I said let's wait till 'ba3deen'.

:: **salam pax 11:43 AM [+]** ::

Sunday, 29 September 2002

The Legendary Monkey needs your suggestions for what she should read next. Show her what you are reading now!

:: **salam pax 2:36 AM [+]** ::

Well . . . as I said, Raed is in Baghdad after a trip to Basra (south of Iraq). He is at the moment crashing on my couch. He wears that T-shirt 24/7. It says MY LIFE IS HAPPY. Yeah, right. And I have a body like Schwarzenegger's.

:: salam pax 2:51 AM [+] ::

Thursday, 3 October 2002

Spiralling down fast. I have been listening to Coldplay's 'Politik' non-stop since 9 a.m. Either the world is not worth commenting on or I am just plain lazy.

:: **salam pax 11:39 AM [+]** ::

Saturday, 5 October 2002

Really had a good weekend. You should have been here. G. called late on Thursday and said he is conducting an experiment with Laurent. It involves three glasses and a bottle of cheap, cheap vodka. I think: 'What the hell? It'll either make me feel worse or it'll make me want to kill myself.' Having prepared razor blades for my wrist-slashing activities at three in the morning, I changed and took a taxi (the driver made me wish I had those blades with me to draw a mark on my wrist every time he bitched about life – 'Stop it, fucker! My blood will be on *your* hands!')

Aaaannnnnnyway. I get to G.'s place with major psychological damage. G. reads books in the correct atmospheric conditions. You know, he once read a book about the tribes of the Arabian desert without having the air-conditioning on (that's, like, 46°C at night!). Now he's reading Rushdie's *Shame* while burning incense and drinking vodka-and-OJ in a coffee mug and wearing his bed sheets like a sarong, which is very much like shame. I love his sense for the theatrical.

Over at Laurent's it is more candlelight and incense (dammit, oriental philanthropists think it's cool . . . Give me L'eau D'Issey air-freshener NOW!) and lots of vodka in glasses which don't stand straight. That was very unsettling. Never do that to someone in a place with too much incense, especially when they're in a suicidal mood. The glasses have a sloping bottom and I'm thinking 'Why won't my drink settle in my glass??' Is that what you see when you are ready to die?? After the third drink it doesn't matter anymore and we are in the middle of the most insane discussions. Around 2 a.m. Laurent demonstrates how ARAK burns with a beautiful blue flame and downs a small glass of the stuff, just like that. I'm thinking 'Eeewww! I can't even smell arak.' After that he demands that we all go to ZarZur's and have kebabs (Note: ZarZurs was closed twice for not abiding to basic health regulations – I worry that dying of food poisoning is not as dramatic as slashing your wrists, but the thought evaporates). Next we have a drunk – really drunk – French dude driving us thru Baghdad, while we discuss cultural imperialism. He almost drives us thru the gates of one of the presidential palaces and the two Iraqi passengers scream in panic, while the two non-Iraqis think we are hilarious and laugh. The discussion goes on at ZarZur's. The waiters like us so much we get all the extra salad we ask for.

Back at Laurent's there's still some alcohol to go thru and it is at that point things start getting interesting: G. knows a guy who is selling these Sumerian cylindrical clay objects (they're tiny – 5cm max – but they look like the real thing) and coins from the Abbasid era (various caliphs). Nothing costs more than 20 bucks and he has jars full of these things. He says it is from a place near his village. They have used brick from the site to build furnaces – hehehe. Bread baked in ancient Sumerian ovens – go baby go!

A couple of months ago I saw one of these Sumerian thingies sold at eBay for around $400 and it was not authenticated – it only had an expert opinion stating that it looked genuine. After a quick drunken calculation I am filthy rich – beautiful hunks queuing up to give me foot massages . . . Now, if only the Evil_Boss_Creature gives me my paycheck . . .

Home at 6 a.m. and sleep till 2 p.m., dreaming of riches.

You should have been here.

And more good news: I moved from 'Politik' to 'A Smile Upon Your

Face' on Coldplay's album. Three tracks in as many days now –
that's what I call progress!

:: **salam pax 9:45 PM [+]** ::

Sunday, 6 October 2002

Googlefight! Googlefight! Googlefight!+
Raed vs Salam.

Salam wins with a whopping 268,000 hits, compared to Raed's
weak 17,700. Thank you, ladies and gentlemen and goodnight.

and I had to try this++ . . . ouch! they beat the shit out of us . . . how
prophetic . . .

:: **salam pax 2:13 PM [+]** ::

Wednesday, 9 October 2002

Real-Life™ by GOD Inc. is not the greatest software available. The
system crashes whenever I run the damn program . . . The SIMS
are much more fun. Just felt like sharing that.

:: **salam pax 11:57 AM [+]** ::

Thank you for the excellent Counterpunch link. I mean, where else
can you read articles with headlines like: '"After all, he tried to kill
my dad!": Iraq as an American projection.'+++

No, that's not the link to the article, it's a link to L. Monkey's . . .
umm . . . remix. I do think he's right, but the whole thing probably
sounds too biased for many people, and try publishing something
like that in most of Europe and you get ANTI-SEMITISM stamped on
your forehead. But boy, is it fun to read.

+ www.googlefight.com.
++ Salam entered the keywords 'Iraq' and 'USA' into the search engine. 'Iraq' scored
14,300,000, but 'USA' scored 69,900,000.
+++ vaspider.surreally.net.

Now this next article is grrrrrreat. I bet you haven't read something like it during all this media-on-war block party:

> . . . but there is one other little-known scenario, based on the American leadership's theological belief system. Bush, Vice-President Dick Cheney and Attorney-General John Ashcroft are all self-professed Evangelical or Born-Again Christians, and like their co-religionists could well believe in the Bible's end-time prophecies to the letter. *Such Messianic prophecies include the stipulation that before the Messiah can return to earth, there will be a major East–West war* and the Jews must rebuild their temple in Jerusalem.[+]

You see, they are preparing for the return of the Messiah. It's the end of days scenario, stupid!

I wonder if anyone has bought the film rights yet?

:: salam pax 12:35 PM [+] ::

Hey. I have exceeded my bandwidth limit again.

Raed, see what you have done by not paying for my image-hosting account. I can't live on 5MB a day . . .

:: salam pax 1:30 PM [+] ::

Thursday, 10 October 2002

For how much would you sell your kidney?

Salah sold his for $250. His fiancée sold hers as well, for the same price. They've been engaged for a while and they needed the $500 (that's equivalent to a million Iraqi dinars) to build two extra rooms in his parents' house for them to live in. I know this because a relative of mine was the buyer.

Breathe in. Change the subject.

Just in case you didn't know, next Sunday is Zacharia's Day; just so

---

[+] 'Might Sharon Nuke Iraq? How Things Could Go Bad, *Very* Bad' (2 October 2002) by Linda S. Heard at www.counterpunch.org.

that you can all get yourselves ready. You know . . . John the Baptist's father. The same story as in the Bible is in the Koran. No-kids-old-guy gets a surprise package via the heavenly express and what does he find? A boy! So, if a woman wishes for a boy on Zacharia's Day and gets one she gives thanks by fasting on that day and giving candles to boys and Arabic drums (*tablas*) to girls. Not exactly subtle symbolism, eh?

And do you know how the wishes are made? You get a boy's candle and stick a needle in it. Ouch. How fast can you say 'penis-envy'? And since my mother has been 'blessed' twice, she has this big do every year. I personally think she's been cheated. I can't see her pricking that candle really hard and thinking 'A heretic idiot, pleeeeez.' Does Mr Z. give refunds?

So boys and girls, get those candles and needles ready. I tell you, I'm hiding my candle where no one but me will be sticking any needles in it – get your own candle you evil witch, this one is mine. I wonder, if I start sticking the needles in it now will the boys be delivered by Sunday? Well, it doesn't hurt to try.

My weekend starts here – and my religious beliefs don't allow me to blog on a Friday.

Raed, you'd better have a comment on each and every single entry you've missed the last couple of days – or a good explanation e-mailed NOW! If Tota is there and has you tied to the bed, you're already forgiven.

Tell her Salam says Hi.

:: **salam pax** 5:00 PM [+] ::

Saturday, 12 October 2002

> **The White House is developing a detailed plan to install an American-led military government in Iraq if the United States topples Saddam Hussein. The plan also calls for a transition to an elected civilian government that could take months or years.[+]**

[+] 'US Has a Plan to Occupy Iraq, Officials Report' (11 October 2002) by David E. Sanger and Eric Schmitt, in the *New York Times* (www.nytimes.com).

Excuse me. But don't expect me to buy little American flags to welcome the new colonists. This is really just a bad remake of an even
worse movie. And how does it differ from Iraq and Britain circa
1920? The civilized world comes to give us, the barbaric nomadic
Arabs, a lesson in better living and rid us of all evil (better still, get
rid of us Arabs since we're all evil).

Yeah, go ahead. Just flush all the efforts of people who were sin-
cere in their fight for an independent Iraq down the drain. People
fought, demonstrated and died so that my generation gets to see all
their dreams turned upside down – twice. First by You-Know-Who
and the second time by becoming a colony all over again.

God, I feel sorry for anyone who has ever had an ideal and fought
for it. I feel sorry for every revolutionary Iraqi who ever wrote a book
or a poem and got executed because of it. If they'd only known that
this was going to happen – that it would all just end up being another colony – they wouldn't have bothered. It's much better to spend
your time on sex, drugs and belly dancers. Uncle Sam is going to
come and tell you how to run a country properly and how to spend
your money on weapons from him – 'Don't go buying useless
Chinese technology, habibi.'

> **It would put an American officer in charge of Iraq for a year or more
> while the United States and its allies searched for weapons and
> maintained Iraq's oil fields. For as long as the coalition partners
> administered Iraq, they would essentially control the second largest
> proven reserves of oil in the world, nearly 11 per cent of the total. A
> senior administration official said the United Nations oil-for-food
> program would be expanded to help finance stabilization and recon-
> struction.[+]**

[uncle_sam_unit]: I told you not to worry about the cost, baby, you'll
    pay for it.

[salam]: Do I have a choice, Sam? Say, what if I don't like what
    you're doing?

[uncle_sam_unit]: No, you don't have a choice and I'm telling you
    you'll *love* it !

What is truly ironic is that the Bush administration is using the same

----
[+] See note on previous page.

argument that Saddam used to invade Kuwait for their invasion of Iraq. 'National security concerns' and 'helping the poor bastards over there to get rid of that evil government'. At least try to be original. I tell you it is about greed and power – it always is. Me and you are only a future statistic. The question is, in which column will we be listed: DEAD or INJURED?

:: salam pax 8:06 PM [+] ::

Tuesday, 15 October 2002

Raed sent a long e-mail (i.e. more than five words) saying that this is turning into a war-blog and he doesn't like it. So, I am toning things down; because if he doesn't like me anymore, I'll actually have to pay for accommodation when I'm next in Jordan and I would like to go there for a week before getting blasted out of the solar system.

First, I want to tell you that I am a happy YES voter. I didn't really read what was written on the piece of paper, but I know the answer is YES. And the whole voting centre I went to also knows I have ticked the YES box, because, you see, I had forgotten my glasses and I needed someone to show me which box to mark for the affirmative. This was asked loud enough for everyone to hear – no need for booths or secrecy.

Outside they were already celebrating, although the voting centres had only just opened. They had sweets and dates and cinnamon-flavoured tea. Personally, I prefer my *chai* flavoured with mint leaves and they had *no* coffee! (I need coffee – at home my family is always hiding the coffee from me. I need caffeine.) So, I stood there for a while watching kids with plastic flowers jump around. We have the day off and I didn't want to go back home, because since last Saturday the house feels like a dorm.

At first it was OK. They were just here to help my mother with this Zacharia's Day thing. Now I have a tiny cousin playing video games downstairs; another watching WWF smackdown videos upstairs; another studying in my bedroom; and still another at my computer browsing thru Saudi discussion boards with subjects like 'What does the man of your dreams look like?'

Last night, while wondering whether to watch semi-naked muscle-men wrestle or tell 'whisper of the night' what the man of my dreams looks like, I realized that I really needed to get loaded.

A quick call to cousin No. 246 (yes I have far too many – my mother has eight sisters and brothers) and he's OK with it, but we have to hurry because all off-licence stores close by 10 p.m. and there are no bars/clubs/restaurants where drinks are served (in addition to that, no alcohol on Fridays, religious holidays and, most distressingly, the whole month of Ramadan).

We get to our friendly Satan's Beverages Dealer just as he is turning his lights off. He sees the desperation in my eyes, smiles, and tells us that he has no local beer left, only imported stuff. Man, I haven't been paid in two months. I don't want to buy imported, give me cheap local poison. Satan's Beverages Dealer just smiles. I buy whatever he has and look at his son. He's not more than seven years old and is drinking Laziza, a non-alcoholic beer. Now what is that kid doing with Laziza? His father looks at him with amusement as the tiny Satan smashes the bottle on the pavement. I can't deal with this any longer. I go hide in the car while my cousin is giving Satan's Beverages Dealer his money. Tiny Satan waves goodbye.

Blast fills the screen.

Fade to black.

Credits.

:: **salam pax 2:37 PM [+]** ::

Wednesday, 16 October 2002

I am very impressed! Jim Henley's website Unqualified Offerings: War, Peace, Freedom, Fish, More[+] has a very well-informed source. Now, let's see if his source can tell him what happened to the phonelines since Monday. Back to you, Mr Henley.

:: **salam pax 12:53 PM [+]** ::

[+] Unqualified Offerings ('Peace Now! Socialism never!'): www.highclearing.com.

Thursday, 17 October 2002

By some unthinkable means, Diana[*] manages to make me tell her things I shouldn't. I just can't help myself. And look where it got me. Today she sends me this link from the *Los Angeles Times* and asks if the tribal leader they talk about is my grandad:

> **Shwerid serves as a mediator in disputes, both civil and criminal. Although he is careful not to place himself above national law, his followers often turn to him, rather than the Iraqi courts, to resolve disputes.[**]**

Before you read the rest of the paragraph, please bear this in mind: national law is a farce because of the corruptibility of the system. People don't bother to call the police when there's trouble, because they'll just write the report in favour of whoever pays the most. Now you can gasp at what comes next:

> **For example, if one person kills another on purpose, Shwerid will order the aggressor to pay the victim's family $7,000 in blood money.**

Now *that* is a lie. Shame on you, Shwerid – and you call yourself a tribal leader . . .

Well, if *you* pay $7,000 in blood money, that's just because you're a foreigner and they always get inflated prices. Get someone local to bargain for you and you'll get away with paying only $1,000 – $2,000 max. Really. Unless you were really bad and shot someone very important in the tribe – the leader's son for example. Then you'll have to pay four times as much as the amount you would have to pay for killing a regular Joe.

Now before you start your rants and flames and angry disgusted e-mails, please remember what I wrote above. The law has very little influence deep in rural areas and this is meant to be a deterrent, not a pay-per-kill scheme.

----
[*] Diana at Letter from Gotham: letterfromgotham.blogspot.com.
[**] From an article in the *LA Times* (www.latimes.com).

Back to sheikh Shwerid:

> 'Yes, we will resist anyone who comes here, using our own weapons,' Shwerid said, while seated inside a guest house he uses to greet tribal members who travel from around the country seeking his help and advice. 'The tribe is fully co-operating with the Government.'

Of course, by 'here' Shwerid means his and the tribe members' land. It has nothing to do with the Government. These people live off the land and it is the most prized possession you can get in Iraq: fertile land. So what do you do when you see a mob of armed people coming towards you? You defend your land, crops and families. And if you are a strong tribe in the area, you keep all the other tribes in check: 'Don't hurt my land and I won't hurt you.' It just happened as a side-effect that the Government benefited from the control these strong tribes exercised in certain areas. But the government quickly realized the potential and 'nurtured them, winning their good favor with money and supplies' – and gave them fancy cars imported as part of the food for oil programme.

By Allah, she made me do it again! OK, I have *not* told you this.

Diana, in answer to your question: no, this is not my grandad. But sheikh Shwerid sure makes me feel like a 'bargain-basement' person. I hope no one hears we come that cheap per shot. My tribal leader has to get his pricing policy up to date and fast.

:: **salam pax 3:42 AM [+]** ::

A German scientist thinks that he can tell which of the Saddams are the fake ones and which is the real. This was reported on German television around the 26th of September. Check it on msnbc.com, news24.com or (where they really got into the spirit of the report and started looking for *doppelgängers* everywhere) at FM4 discussion boards – it's in German.

To demonstrate this amazing ability to analyse facial features, the *New York Times* has put up this interactive thingy.[+] Go check it. It's

----
[+] 'Will the Real Saddam Hussein Please Step Down?' (6 October 2002) by Tom Zeller (www.nytimes.com).

a joke. Go to the link which says 'Can you spot Saddam?' and check the answer.

It tells me nothing. Of course the guy looks different than the other pictures, because the one Dr Dieter thinks is the real deal was shot sometime in the early 1970s, while the other three are very recent photos (as in this-year/last-year recent). Can't they allow a guy to grow and wrinkle a bit? Yes he might have doubles, but Dr Dieter proved nothing.

:: **salam pax 1:42 PM [+]** ::

Sunday, 20 October 2002

> **'We'll happily watch the American bullets fly over our heads at first,' said one disgruntled intellectual. 'But after a two-year honeymoon we'll be shooting at them. Iraqis will never, ever be ruled by foreigners.'[+]**

I'm afraid most Iraqis fail to understand what will be brought about by an American 'invasion'. It should be seen as a catalyst for change. We have to do the hard work ourselves. Change has to come from within. It's no use just sitting back and waiting for others to solve our problems. And Iraq will be ruled by foreigners if Iraqis don't take an active part in whatever happens. The problem is that years of being told what to do has turned us into a bunch of fatalists who see whatever happens to us as *maktub* – written by the hand of God – and submit to it, like all good faithful people should.

FunFact of the day: when was the last time the Iraqi 'man-in-the-street' had the right to express an honest and free opinion about the Government's policies?

Answer: 1962. That's forty years ago.

I can only hope that our American friends don't forget to bring extra copies of *Democracy for Dummies* and *Make a Decision: It's Not as Hard as it Sounds* with them.

The quote above is taken from an article in *The Economist*. You

----

+ 'Waiting, with bravado and anxiety' (17 October 2002) in *The Economist* (economist.com).

should go and read it. What I really like about the article is that it reads like a How Iraqis Feel Today guide. It's all here . . .

The bitterness brought on by years of sanctions and poverty:

> 'Assuming I were to say I don't like our president, I still believe many of his positions are just,' said a Baghdad accountant-turned-taxi-driver. 'Do Americans think forcing me to look for fares, just so I can send my children to school wearing shoes, is just?'

The effect of years and years of propaganda (and believe me, it works – you won't discuss something that became a 'fact' after having it hammered into your head time after time. You don't think. You have learned all the answers by heart without even knowing it):

> The hostility to America, echoed by a range of Iraqis, from a successful Baghdad sculptor to a village share-cropper, is understandable. Relentlessly repeated footage of Israeli brutality, often juxtaposed with images of 'collateral damage' from American bombing in Afghanistan and in Iraq's 'no-fly zones', fill the state-controlled airwaves.

The fear of seeing old grudges resurface if the country falls into chaos:

> The small Christian minority, fairly prosperous but decimated by emigration, worries that without the protection of the secular Baathists, the Muslim religious revival which has swept the country could turn against them. Sunni Muslims, who are over-represented in government but vastly outnumbered by the Shia, fear losing their traditional dominance. Loyalists in the Baath Party and in dozens of Arab tribes – including Shia as well as Sunni clans – fear retribution.

Actually, I don't get the 'secular Baathists' part. The Muslim religious revival is heavily sponsored by the Party.+ Whatever.

+ The word 'Baath' means 'Renaissance' in Arabic. The original Arab Socialist Baath Party was founded in Syria in the 1940s. The Iraqi Baath Party was founded in 1951. Saddam Hussein joined it in 1956 and the Party came to power on 8 February 1963 in a coup backed by the army, overthrowing Brigadier Abdel Karim Qasim (who had previously overthrown the British-installed Iraqi monarchy in 1958). Saddam Hussein was elected Assistant General Secretary of the Party in 1966 and staged a successful coup in 1968. From 1979 to 2003 he was the President, Head of the Revolutionary Command Council and Secretary General of the Baath Party.

And finally, a general discontent at how bad things have become:

> Baghdad, once a city of broad avenues, villas and European-standard public housing, now looks more like Kinshasa, Congo's sad capital, complete with lakes of sewage, piles of trash, beggars and straggling flea markets.

I usually have more fun when I can disagree with western journalists. Maybe if I read it again I can find something.

Totally off the subject: I am compiling a Top Five list of my favourite Iraqi anti-Bush slogans in English. At the moment I have two competing for the top spot: 'Bush Go Hell!' and 'Down Down Bush and his Tail Blair!'

:: salam pax 1:56 AM [+] ::

> Last March, Arraf published a piece in London's *Daily Telegraph* [in which] she wrote: 'People in the streets are not allowed to talk to television journalists; or rather, the journalists are not allowed to talk to them. "Why do you want to ask them political questions? They are not qualified to answer," an official said . . .'+

Well . . . if this is true, why are British journalists interviewing people up and down the country? It looks like you're going to bump into a British journalist just by standing in the street. *The Economist* has an article with interviews and here are two more from the *Guardian* website: '"But why do they hate us?" Iraqis face up to the threat of a US attack' and 'X marks the despot: Bombing Iraq into democracy could well prove counterproductive'.++

I demand to be interviewed. I'm going to stand all day in Arasat Street, because Mr Rory McCarthy seems to be spending a lot of time there, he knows so much about it:

> The shops in Baghdad's Arasat Street reek of the opulence of corrupt Third World élites. Wide-screen televisions sell for hundreds of pounds alongside shops that specialise in original chrome parts for

----

+ From an article in *The New Republic* (ssl.com).

++ '"But why do they hate us?" Iraqis face up to the threat of a US attack' (20 October 2002) by Rory McCarthy. 'X marks the despot: Bombing Iraq into democracy could well prove counterproductive' (16 October 2002) by Brian Whitaker (www.guardian.co.uk).

Toyota Land Cruisers. Supermarkets sell foreign cigarettes and under-the-counter Cuban cigars at £100 a box. Every other car on the road is a new BMW or Mercedes-Benz. All this in a country in which UN sanctions have supposedly strictly limited imports to humanitarian goods alone.

Yeah. And there's a single yellow new VW Beetle that cruises that street as well. Actually it's probably just as well that Mr McCarthy stays in Arasat Street, foreigners seem to develop strange ailments if they eat anywhere else.

:: **salam pax 11:35 AM [+]** ::

Tuesday, 22 October 2002

I should write something about this, but I can't.+ So the amnesty states that all political prisoners can go. So where is H.? They said that this amnesty should leave no one in prison within 48 hours, so where is he? I want him to be at home, safe. I can't keep calling his brother only to hear that there is still no news.

:: **salam pax 4:00 AM [+]** ::

Wednesday, 23 October 2002

Raed, I'm sorry but David Bowie's song 'I'm Afraid of Americans' is stuck in my head and I can't think of anything else to write.

Actually . . . there is a lot to write about, but it doesn't matter. H. is not home yet. From what I have heard today I should brace myself for bad news. Political prisoners have been dealt with. Light a candle for me will you, Raed? Keeping myself together takes effort the last two days.

And forget about the trip to Amman. You asked about what is happening at the Jordanian border a couple of days ago. Well, Jordanians are not letting thru any Iraqi under the age of fifty. Guess why? Because the American and the Israeli army are play-

----

+ 'Saddam sets free political prisoners' (21 October 2002) by Rory McCarthy (www.guardian.co.uk).

ing war games in the western (well, eastern for Jordan) desert. And the Jordanians are bending over to make sure that the Amis are getting as deep as they want to. Yeah, me-love-you-long-time – no need for lube either. The war hasn't started and we are already imprisoned in Iraq. Jordan isn't letting anyone thru its borders and neither is Iran (look for it yourself. I can't be bothered. I read it in the *New York Times* a couple of days ago) and do you know what else I read in the *New York Times*? The American troops they are studying how the Israeli army fought in Jenin.

Jenin. Remember how Jenin looked like after the siege? How comforting is that?

Excuse me, but I need to listen to some angry-boy-music and bang my head against a wall and bleed; it will make me feel better, I'm sure. Have I told you already that I hate the world?

P.S. Raed, don't even think about coming to Baghdad the next couple of days/weeks. You might not be able to go back to Jordan. Besides, I don't want you here the next couple of days. I am planning on spending them in a drunken haze. I do not want you near me.

Love,

Salam

:: salam pax 4:13 AM [+] ::

Draft of the US-British Resolution on Iraq: ' . . . in order to restore international peace and security.'

Peace and Security. Ha.

Bomb us, already. Stop pussyfooting.

:: salam pax 11:56 AM [+] ::

Thursday, 24 October 2002

Today I am not going to read *any* news and I'm only going to watch *So 80's* on VH1 – *and* tell you about things that made me smile.

1. Reading the e-mails I got from the Legendary Monkey, Kashei✦ and Diana. Thank you. Warm fuzzies have never felt better.

2. Having one of my posts chosen as 'Slogan of the Day' on Samizdata.net and receiving the 'dubious honour of a permanent link'. Expect a lot of blog-related terminology in the future. Fear my blog-cabulary.✦✦

3. E-mail from Joe Schmo of www.boredshitless.com asking Who-the-hell-are-you?-type questions. You'll get your answers but, believe me, Diana will still know more – she has ways. Is 'tele-hypnosis' a word? Joe has added me to the links on his blog. I am one of the new links and so is Letter from Gotham [letterfrom-gotham.blogspot.com] (that does make me feel kinda special).

4. My younger brother deciding to start his own groupblog with a couple of friends around the world. I have finally corrupted him. Now I can pretend that I am not reading his weblog, just like he pretends he doesn't read mine. A BLOG FOR EVERY IRAQI! – that will be my campaign slogan.

5. The secretary at the office finally stopped hiding the solitaire game she is playing on her computer after I showed her my favourite online silly games. Next step is to stage a demonstration against the oppressive rule of Evil_Boss_Unit.

:: **salam pax 1:30 PM [+]** ::

Sunday, 27 October 2002

Looking thru the *New York Times* e-mail alerts I see this: '12 Americans Stage Protest Hussein Is Happy to Allow'.✦✦✦ I read thru it wondering if Mr JOHN F. BURNS is reporting news from the same Baghdad I live in. Nothing in the news about it and no one at work making any look-at-those-poor-deluded-souls-going-at-it-again comments (which is one of two responses to this sort of thing – the other being 'I wonder how much money are they getting as a

----

✦ www.alarmingnews.com, hosted by Kashei and Peter.
✦✦ www.samizdata.net/blog/glossary.html.
✦✦✦ An article by John F. Burns, 27 October 2002 (www.nytimes.com).

"thank-you" gift from Saddam?'). Half-way thru the article Mr Burns does say that there was virtually no Iraqi media present at the 'protest'. Right on. Ms Kelly might as well have staged that protest in her bathroom.

Dear American friends, please stop sending her over here. She is not helping. Some people might think that this is the sort of thing I like to see happening. It is NOT. Kelly, baby, you have been used. They have put you on show for the westerners. For me, personally, I lost interest when you were quoted saying things like: 'I wish people in our country would be willing to show the same *spirit of forgiveness and reconciliation* to the two million people in our prisons.'

I think you'd better take your 'thank-you' gift and leave. Fast. It feels like you're stepping on my toes. And I pray for 'your' prisoners that they are not shown the exact same 'spirit of (no-trial-just-shoot-them-I-don't-want-to-worry-about-them) forgiveness'.

I would have loved to shake you by the hand and give you a 'thank-you' hug, but that statement . . . tsk tsk tsk.

Is she really that naive or just trying to stay on the right side of the red line? I would forgive her for the latter. Everybody has to make a living, somehow.

:: salam pax 7:10 PM [+] ::

Tuesday, 29 October 2002

Which is sexier? To be a CIA put-up or a propaganda ploy?

A week ago Kathy K. of On the Third Hand [site-essential.com] linked to a post on my site and at the end of her comments about the post she wrote 'I've been watching him for a while, and I think he's real.'

I linked back to her, saying 'I'm for real. Really.'

Actually, almost everyone who has linked to me either wrote in their weblog that they wonder if it is for real or e-mailed me asking – with the exception of the Legendary Monkey. That's because she is Legendary. She just *knows*.

But Al from Culpepper Log[+] thought the whole issue of my 'real-ness' was worth writing about. So over to you Al:

. . . [*the blog*] **fascinates me on a couple of general grounds. First, I'm damned curious what people in Iraq (and the whole Middle East, for that matter) really think of the US. [. . .] Do they mostly even kind of half believe the Baath Party American Satan thing?** [*Well, we did have another Satan. During the 1980s Ayatollah Khomeini was the Shaitan before America, but now we are friends with Iran so America gets to be the new Shaitan. Very Orwellian, eh?*]

Do they anxiously await us to come 'liberate' them, as our govern-ment generally insists they will? [*Oh-oh . . . did he say 'liberate'?*] **Raed seems to welcome our prospective liberation** [*whaaa? Which part of my rant wasn't clear enough and please don't use that word again it hurts*] **– if perhaps with some trepidation. 'Ha. Bomb us already. Stop pussyfooting.'** [*That post was meant to be sarcastic, or do you really believe that resolution will restore international peace and security? And there is more . . .*] **The site looks believable. Also, however, I WANT to believe.** [*Here he links to the X-Files site – he also thinks I'm from planet K-Pax, apparently.*] **This alone makes me a little suspicious. They have a somewhat cynical and fatalistic tone that I'd find likely. There are cryptic personal notes.** [*These notes are not cryptic. This is Arablish. Because most of the world thinks that communication revolves around the English language we have to adapt our language to these non-Arabic enabled systems. Ya3ni lo a77*i inglizi lo 2aba6il.*][++] **The use of the English language is convinc-ingly rough.** [*Oh maaan, I have been told numerous times that my Arabic is rough. I know my German is rough and now my English is rough. I blame my parents for moving me around every five years. I need a mother tongue. Should I try Esperanto??*] **But does that really mean that it's real? If someone at the CIA were trying to con-struct a convincing fake Iraqi website for our domestic consumption, it would probably look somewhat like this.** [*Excuse my rough English, but what 'consumption'?? I average 20 hits a day on a good week, unless Instapundit links to me or – ohmigod – Instapundit is the CIA too!*] **If 'Raed' is a fake, it's a fairly convincing one.** [*Raed, baby, I always knew you were a fake. Salam rules. Yeah!*]

[+] Al Barger, host of Culpepper Log: www.morethings.com/log/.

[++] 'You mean I either speak English or nothing at all'.

At least he gets one thing right:

> **He can't really be expected to prove himself. He's writing stuff that would get him shot in a second if Hussein's goons found him.**

What you really missed is that I am not Raed. Look again at who is posting. You didn't even bother to do that? Well, it happens when one is too concerned about conspiracy theories and the like.

One more correction, neither I nor Raed are 'regular Joes'. Actually most regular Joes would look at us suspiciously. I have spent half of my life out of this country and had to be taught how to re-grow my roots by someone who isn't even Iraqi by nationality, he just loves the place (thank you, Raed). We both have a mistrust of religion and have read the *Tao Te Ching* with more interest than the Koran. And we both have mouths which have gotten us into trouble. The regular Joe would be more inclined to beat the shit out of us infidels.

Go ask Diana. She knows.

UPDATE: letterfromgotham.blogspot.com also comes to the rescue: 'bloggadavit about the authenticity of one Salam Pax of Baghdad.'

:: salam pax 5:15 PM [+] ::

Saturday, 2 November 2002

The Theory and Practice of Gossip:

What to do on the last weekend before the 'holy' month of Ramadan?

Make sure I have enough alcohol stashed away and let the Shallowness shine for one last time (i.e. catch up on the latest rumours making the rounds in the circles of ill-repute before they adjourn for a month and turn religious). Tempted by Z.'s promise that he'll introduce me to his new friend (what better gossip material than that?), I spent Thursday night with people whom I have nothing in common with. My head is full of unconnected, useless information about cars and weapons. It turns out Z.'s new squeeze is an expert in all sorts of guns.

I mean, whoever heard of a fag dealing in weapons? It's supposed to be decorators, hair-stylists and the occasional unsuccessful architect – ahem ahem – right? Stick to your stereotypes please. It makes you better targets.

Talking of targets, here is FunFact No. 1:
The black market price of a locally produced bullet for your lovingly customized AK-47 is 35 Iraqi dinars – that's less than two cents or cheaper than the price of one chemically flavoured Iraqi lollipop. Go suck on a bullet kid.

So, let's start the gossip marathon.

I guess that by now it is clear why the foreign reporters were chucked out of the country. How on earth could they report on something that never happened? Of course we wouldn't trust journalists who fabricate news. Today this, tomorrow – who knows what? I really feel sorry for the poor bastards in the Ministry of Information. You can't even imagine what sort of panic they must have been thru. Reports of demonstrations; dissent among the Iraqi people a few days after the 100 per cent vote; western journalists reporting about such a distasteful event: 'Yalla yalla, throw those reporters out quick before they get us executed!' Another mess and more reports about the oppressive Iraqi 'regime' (put that word in your report and your visa will magically expire). Typical Iraqi impulsiveness. But the Government is not full of idiots, so a few days later and they try to act all flirty again. According to the *New York Times*:

> **A flurry of enhanced amiability at the official media center in Baghdad, headquarters for visiting reporters, appeared to be part of a wider effort by President Hussein to present a more moderate image to the world in the face of American war threats. All day, officials set out to counter reports that they were moving to expel members of CNN's Baghdad bureau, along with many other Western reporters, after the wide coverage given last week to scattered Baghdad street protests.**[+]

Imagine yourself the Iraqi Minister of Information and try to explain this to Mr President: CNN's Baghdad bureau used its satellite dish to broadcast live coverage of the demonstration. Less significant blunders than this got ministers out of their chairs and out of this world.

FunFact No. 2:
For $200 you can get a nice Iraqi-made gun. It's called Tarek (6ari8 for you Arablish speakers). And if you manage to smuggle one thru the Saudi border, they'll trade it in for a new Toyota pick-up truck. Very big with farmers.

Update on the Jordanian border issue: the age is 40 not 50. Under that age no Iraqi male will be allowed to enter Jordan, unless he can prove that he already has an airplane ticket to another country and will be given a transit visa for ten days. Or he is part of the oil

----
[+] 'Threats and responses: foreign correspondents' (28 October 2002) by John. F. Burns (www.nytimes.com).

smuggling trade. In that case it's 'Drive right thru, Mr Oil Tank Driver.' Go on, treat us like shit. It's not like you're the only ones.

King Abdullah you are freaking me out. Look at this from arabic news.com:*

> **The Jordanian King Abdullah II does not rule out that Iraq will be one day ruled by a member of the Hashamite family.**

So now you want your share of the pie?

One word: VULTURES!

He stressed that Jordan is 'neutral and any request from it for American protection might be understood as an aggressive step against Iraq.'

Sorry. Not 'understood', but *is*. Jordan is not exactly loved by Iraqis lately, so you better watch it. You have been bad to the Iraqis there, so don't expect us to treat you like royalty here.

FunFact No. 3:
One day after the prisons were emptied the Ministry of Internal Affairs made a record number of arrests: 400 in a single day. Charges varied from assault to theft.

I don't have to pay 400k Iraqi dinars ($200) to get permission to travel abroad any more (one trip, valid for one year as of stamp date). But where am I to go? Forget about western countries. I am asking about visas to neighboring countries.

Kuwait? Heehee. Next.

Iran? And get your name tagged by the intelligence service? They won't give you a visa anyway.

Turkey? Forget it, they make you wait and then tell you sorry.

Jordan? Nope. Male under 40.

Syria? Disco! My next holiday is the explore-Syria-tour. The question is, when are they going to join the fence-in-the-Iraqis club? Other members of this club include Lebanon and Egypt.

----
* www.arabicnews.com.

It seems that the fourteen controlled satellite channels project (called the rafidain network) is a total flop. Out of 10,000 decoders only 6,000 were sold, and this in a city with around five million inhabitants. This needs a little explaining. Installing a satellite TV dish in your house is punishable by 750,000 Iraqi dinars and three months in prison. But two months ago the Government decided to re-transmit fourteen selected channels, hand-picked with the assistance of the ART network. The ART channels get the biggest share – National Geographic and Discovery are also part of the batch, and one western music channel, which the newspapers attack because of the loose morals such channels spread. Lately they have decided to change Animal Planet to the Paramount Comedy Channel. Now we watch *Seinfeld* and *Dharma & Greg*. But Mr Channel Zapper hates Jay Leno, because at 10 p.m. they change the channel to TCM (they even do the channel-surfing for you – do they love us or what?). The service is only available in Baghdad and is a phenomenal failure. According to a call-in radio show, the main reasons why people didn't subscribe to the service was that it's outside the range of the average budget, many find the choice of channels unattractive (the ART network isn't exactly the most attractive package) and there are no news channels.

I think by now we all agree that I talk too much and need someone to take the keyboard away from me.

:: **salam pax 3:40 PM [+]** ::

Monday, 4 November 2002

Kuwait joins the toss-them-out club. What are those creepy journalists doing in our countries?

I suggest we totally stop having journalism courses in our universities. Shaitan is speaking thru them. I'm sure we can find a Koranic verse somewhere to back me up on this.

It seems al-Jazeera is having serious trouble keeping its mouth shut. The BBC says: 'It has also run into problems with its reporting in Iraq and Saudi Arabia, and both Jordan and Bahrain have banned the station from operating on their soil.'

This is the second time in less than thirty days that they've managed to get their offices closed in an Arabic country. Keep it up, boys and girls. I am thinking of a new marketing slogan for you: 'Al-Jazeera: the only Arabic news network with no offices in the Arabic world.'

:: **salam pax 10:47 AM [+]** ::

Here's something from the BBC News:**+**

> **Kuwait has cordoned-off a large area of the country near the Iraqi border for the duration of *joint US-Kuwait military exercises* . . . a less well-publicised special forces exercise has also been under way in Jordan.**

Dear Kuwait,
Thank you for being clear and honest about it, not like other people who are too wussy to admit they are:
a) scared
b) don't like us any more
c) want a piece of Iraq pie.
Because coming out like that would mean they won't get $500 million in subsidized oil a year.

:: **salam pax 12:17 PM [+]** ::

Tuesday, 5 November 2002

Diana moves thru the web in mysterious ways.

She linked to another wacky Iraqi (actually *the* Wacky Iraqi – he has the papers and domain name to prove it).**++** He had elections on the 16th of October and has an excellent online journal as well.

Diana, I would like to remind you that you've already promised to give *me* your 200 silk dresses. I don't care how many Wacky Iraqis you find, the dresses are mine.

:: **salam pax 12:14 PM [+]** ::

+ news.bbc.co.uk.
++ The Wacky Iraqi is at www.wackyiraqi.com/home/.

Wednesday, 6 November 2002

Israeli Prime Minister Ariel Sharon said that when the international community finishes dealing with Iraq, it should turn its attention to Iran. Mr Sharon made the comments in an interview with the newspaper the London *Times*.+

sigh

shakes head in disbelief

Mr Sharon labels Iran 'a centre of world terror'. He said Iran is making every effort to acquire weapons of mass destruction that would pose a threat to the Middle East and Europe. The text from the interview actually says 'is a danger to the Middle East, to Israel, and a danger to Europe.'

I wonder what the correct term for Israel's nuclear arsenal is? Weapons of mass love-and-harmony?

Sharon 'considers that Iran is a "centre of world terror", and that as soon as an Iraq conflict is concluded, he will push for Iran to be at the top of the "to do" list.'

:: salam pax 1:20 PM [+] ::

Saturday, 9 November 2002

Z. is in Baghdad wa hia 7amil, ra7 tob8a hna ila an t7*eeb.++ I don't know how wise that is considering the situation.

Did you find yourself or are you still lost?

:: salam pax 2:28 AM [+] ::

Mohammed Aldouri [Iraq's ambassador to the United Nations] **told Reuters that he was 'very pessimistic. This resolution is crafted in such a way to prevent inspectors to return to Iraq,' he told the news agency.+++**

+ From the VOA News website: www.voanews.com.

++ 'She is pregnant, she will stay here until she gives birth'.

+++ An article from the *International Herald Tribune* (9 November 2002) by Terence Neilan (www.iht.com).

Very true. If the resolution was meant to piss off the Iraqi government, then it did a good job. Even if the inspectors were allowed to
return, there are so many traps to fall in and the Iraqi government is
not very well known for its patience. Please go read the draft carefully and see for yourself.

> **3. [. . .] as well as all other chemical, biological, and nuclear pro-
> grams, including any which it claims are for purposes not related to
> weapon production or material . . .**

Expect our universities to be declared 'exclusion zones' by Unmovic
any day now. Not that it didn't happen the time before, when professors were body searched as if they were criminals.

> **4. DECIDES that false statements or omissions in the declarations
> submitted by Iraq pursuant to this resolution [. . .] this resolution
> shall constitute a further material breach of Iraq's obligations and
> will be reported to the Council for assessment in accordance with
> Paragraph 11 or 12 below.**

They forgot to mention typos. 'One spelling mistake and you're
minced *kufta* meat, you Iraqi scum.'

> **5. [. . .] as well as immediate, unimpeded, unrestricted, and private
> access to all officials and other persons whore** [ooooh typo . . . you
> get bombed for that if you are an Iraqi – or are they planning to inter-
> view the Whore of Babylon herself? Please tell them to wait, my
> wardrobe has not arrived yet]. **Unmovic or the IAEA wish to interview
> in the mode or location of Unmovic's or the IAEA's choice, pursuant
> to any aspect of their mandates; further decides that Unmovic and
> the IAEA may at their discretion conduct interviews inside or out-
> side of Iraq, may facilitate the travel of those interviewed and family
> members outside of Iraq . . .**

Now, how likely is it they are going to let that happen? My advice to
Blixy: demand to interview some high government official abroad
the moment you are in Iraq – you'll save everybody a lot of time.

And it goes on and on.

One word floats above my head, speech-bubble-style: 'provocative'.

Meanwhile the Iraqi public is treated like mushrooms by the
Iraqi government: kept in the dark and fed on horse manure.
There's nothing in the Iraqi media about the resolution. While the

Independent declares this to be the day the world turned on Iraq, the taxi-driver taking me home didn't even know the vote on the UN resolution was today. Slap slap! Wake up! They will drag you out tomorrow to walk in a staged protest and you don't even know what you're protesting against. I will go and hold a banner saying WE ARE NOT IDIOTS! This is not a 'final chance to comply', this is America's way to make it look legit. And I won't be alone . . .

> 'Even if Iraq accepts the new resolution, the United States . . . will find a thousand and one ways of using the [UN arms] inspectors to attack Iraq,' predicted Amal Mohammad, a 35-year-old housewife.
>
> 'I was very disappointed when I learned that the US draft was unanimously adopted even though it . . . gives the United States the cover it has long sought to carry out an attack against Iraq,' said Kamel Naim, a 37-year-old translator.[+]

My favourite headline until now is from Reuters: WORLD SEES CHANCE FOR PEACE, IRAQ MUM ON UN VOTE.[++]

Funny, the world sees peace, while I have to prepare a bomb shelter in my house.

If you need me, I'm hiding under my bed until this is over.

:: salam pax 3:34 AM [+] ::

The Actual Wording of the Iraq Resolution (ScrappleFace has better sources than the *New York Times*):

> WHEREAS . . . now, where were we? Oh, yeah . . . whereas the media will never report the details of this resolution, because they'll focus on who won – France or the USA – like it's some kind of Olympic luge competition, and . . .
>
> WHEREAS the UN is pretty desperate to find a *raison d'être* . . .
>
> THEREFORE, BE IT RESOLVED THAT Saddam must eliminate all Weapons of Mass Destruction in Iraq (which he

----
+ ABC News Online: www.abc.net.au/news.
++ See reuters.com.

won't) without delay (which he will) or the UN (really the US) will teach him the definition of the word HELLFIRE.+

This comes via On the Third Hand, run by Kathy K. She was not sure France would back the resolution and I thought Syria would abstain. Shame on you both! After all the 406/306 Peugeots Iraqis have bought. Eh? What to do? You spend lotsa money trying to buy friends and then we end up doing the Brutus/Caesar scene . . . Et tu, Brute?

:: **salam pax 10:36 AM [+]** ::

Wednesday, 13 November 2002

There was a parliament session planned in the morning, but as the MPs arrived they were told that the session was rescheduled for the evening instead, right after Iftar (it is Ramadan after all), unless they were Party members. They had a meeting going on right then. Later, fifty MPs were called to come thirty minutes earlier than the scheduled session. They were informed that they will be speaking during the next two days and the vote will be a unanimous NO to the resolution.

Each member had the right to formulate his own speech, but they were given guidelines about which things to mention. Shockingly enough, it turns out some of the MPs had not even seen the UN resolution until that moment. That's why many of the speeches made were so vague and repetitive. They re-wrote the guidelines with some Koran thrown in for good measure. The media was brought in and the stage set for a fine piece of theatre.

Nobody inside Iraq even bothered to tune in to hear what the parliamentarians had to say, while al-Jazeera thought it was worth live coverage. But the Iraqi government did make it worthwhile for them. Who would have thought that they would reject the resolution? My money was on the Iraqi Parliament accepting the resolution and Saddam reluctantly giving the OK, because that was the 'will of his people'. Now I am very interested in the speech he will make to 'justify' the acceptance of the UN resolution despite the recommenda-

----
+ www.scrappleface.com.

tion of the Iraqi Parliament. (Not that he has to justify anything or listen to recommendations, but since the whole thing was public he will make his views known – he likes to give speeches.)

Another nice twist in the plot was the paper the walking-talking freak show presented on the second day. Of course, he was too busy polishing his guns to present the paper in person. He gets to make the whole parliament look like fools by being so insightful and wise. He bashes Russia, Syria and 'other countries which I will not name' and says something stupid about who is to fire the first shot? 'We shall not wait for the arrows to be shot at us . . . blah blah blah.' I found the paper online – it's on an Iraqi governmental site.

As much as I find the resolution unfair, provocative and unrealistic in its demands and timeline – and vague enough to allow for all sorts of traps – I hope Saddam does accept it. Only to buy us time. It is a lose-lose situation for the Iraqi people no matter how you look at it. The US is still talking of 'regime change'. I think Iraq will not go past the first thirty days before the US shouts 'foul!' And in a case of war, I do believe that if Saddam has any biological or chemical weapons he is very likely to use them on his own people to give CNN and al-Jazeera the bloody images everyone doesn't want to see.

:: salam pax 1:40 AM [+] ::

Thursday, 14 November 2002

This post[+] on Sudden Nothing feels like the mosh-pit in a Nine Inch Nails concert (to tell the truth, I have never been to a NIN concert, nor would I be in the mosh-pit at any concert), but you know how they look like: jumping, shouting and pushing each other. Great fun.

Al Barger of the Culpepper Log – after suggesting that I am a CIA put-up and later 'making friends' (well, everybody is invited to the post-war *chai* party on the rubbles of my house) – is asking the Legendary Monkey: 'Do we bite the bullet now or wait till it gets far worse?'

Come along, we are all jumping up and down and while I am singing (I wish) as loud as I can. Not really.

+ vaspider.surreally.net/suddennothing/archives/001828.html#001828.

AI is even suggesting we move to another venue, because this is so much fun we might as well take it out of the Comments thingy.

:: salam pax 11:44 AM [+] ::

Friday, 15 November 2002

Re: An Open Letter to an Iraqi Citizen**+**

It's OK. Really.

I understand your point. But I also have the right to have a different opinion (well at least here on the Internet) and I can't just sit and say 'Go ahead, bomb away!' Because no matter what you say to me, I will still see what is happening now and the very probable war as part of the USA's on-going process to impose its control abroad. Colonialism isn't the word, but it has the same colour scheme.

Yes, this sounds silly, but look at what the American government is doing thru non-American eyes and you'll see a different picture. It is not only Iraq, but foreign policy in general.

I know the war is inevitable and I know nothing you said was meant as an attack on me personally – and I know Saddam is a nutcase with a finger on the trigger. But this is my country and I love its people. There is no way you can convince me that a war is OK. I worry about what will happen during the attacks and I worry more about what will happen afterwards. I take walks in parts of the old city and I can't stop thinking 'Will this be still there this time next year?' You are right; on an emotional level I cannot and will not accept a war on Iraq. But on the other hand . . .

Look, there is no way I am going to say it, mainly because I do not trust the intentions of the American government.

There is also another point which I hope you are not overseeing. This whole MidEast/Iraq/Islam chaos is not bringing us any closer to peace. The Arabs always had repressive governments and religion is what most people turn to under this repression. The whole issue of demonizing Arabs and Islam, and keeping the region so long on the boil by constantly prodding the sore spots is rubbing

----
+ www.morethings.com.log/.

everybody the wrong way. Keep it up and the USA will have to get into a lot of wars in the region. I personally – although I am not religious and would not choose Islam as a religion even if I were forced to choose one – see myself as a person who belongs to a culture which is Islamic and Arabic and who is very happy with his 'identity' (shut up Raed, I mean it), the constant verbal bashing of Arabs and Muslims does make me uncomfortable. The 'You-started-it' argument will get us nowhere – it goes round and round.

You say:

> I can appreciate how you might not feel very friendly towards President Bush, or to me personally for supporting him in this effort. Please believe me, though, when I say that I have nothing but love in my heart for you and your countrymen. I look forward to the day – which will be coming very soon – when the menace of Hussein and his henchmen is gone from you.

I'll say Amen to that last part, but you won't tell anyone I said that. Bush is defiantly not invited to my *chai* party. But you can come along, bring a friend and we'll talk about war and peace. I'll even make dates-pastry. I'll surprise you (they are better than they sound).

:: salam pax 2:21 PM [+] ::

Thursday, 21 November 2002

The Internet connection has been more than irregular in Iraq for almost a week now. We did get a message from the Iraqi service provider stating that they have problems with the satellite link to 'the provider abroad' (i.e. France), but they promised that they will have the problem solved by the 19th. If we can get a connection, it is slow and comes in ten-minute bursts or less. I am browsing non-electronic media. But today it looks like they have solved the problem.

Evil_Boss_Creature, in an attempt to get removed from my hate-list, decided to bribe me with a book: *Targeting Iraq* by Geoff Simons. It is published by Al-Saqi, an Arabic-owned publishing house and bookshop in Britain (it is Iraqi, I think, but I'm not sure. They have published a large number of books by Iraqis, but this could be because most of the authors who matter are banned in Iraq and Al-Saqi is giving them a chance). I used to buy a lot of books from them when I was living abroad. One of the most memorable books was *Republic of Fear* – apparently students in the University of California can access the book online, lucky bastards – and a couple of very good books on Al-Sayab. (While Googling around for al-Sayab, I found someone who has translated my favourite Sayab poem into English as 'The Rain Song'. Try reading it in Arabic. As all Muslim bloggers write: all translations of the Koran are inherently flawed. Very true. 'The Rain Song' sounds much more depressing in Arabic.)

God, those were the days. Just pick up the phone and order a book. Now if I am not travelling I have to be satisfied with second-hand books or photocopies. I am not getting into a discussion about copyrights – it is either that or I can afford nothing to read. I can't even get these photocopies easily, since they don't have the approval seal of the Ministry of Information.

Six months ago the Ministry of Information issued a ruling stating that anyone selling books or photocopies of books without having the ministry's approval will be imprisoned and fined a truckload of money. I go almost every Friday, but there is nothing new. I am still hoping to find that translated copy of Salman Rushdie's *Shame* I saw ages ago.

Anyway, back to Evil_Boss_Creature.

Every time he is in Baghdad I work like a slave because of his hectic schedule and since I am not getting paid properly I make him feel guilty about it. This time he decided bribery will make me get him off the guilt-trip. He was right. *Targeting Iraq* costs exactly 1/8th of my paycheck. I am so fucking cheap.

In other news:

The Iraqi ISP✦ decided that in addition to not allowing any e-mail attachments larger than 500k, we are not allowed to send an e-mail to more than five recipients at a time. Actually this was done in stages; first they limited the number to fifty, then two days ago to five – this was done without any sort of announcement. But

----
✦ Internet Service Provider.

because Raed's brother has such a huge mailing list, he finds these things out. Now he can't tell the world of his latest Flash tricks, and my mailbox (when I am able to open it again) will feel happier.

Babil, the newspaper which has Uday* as chief editor, has been suspended. Last Thursday it published a list of names of various officials and military people who might be interviewed by the inspection team. It was on the last page and made the paper sell like the hot cakes of Bab-al-agha. I have no idea where the walking-talking freak show got the names from, but his papa is very upset about it. So he gives him a slap on the hand.

This is not the first time Uday's paper gets into trouble. He listens to no advice and no adviser will ever challenge anything he says. He has a reputation of shooting people who annoy him in the foot and you don't want to get on the bad side of someone who keeps tigers as pets, unless you fancy yourself as a gladiator.

Anyway, Iraqi journalism is not losing one of its pillars, because *Babil* produces no content of its own. It exploits the relative inaccessibility of the Internet to Iraqis and copies & pastes news from various Arabic news sites.

So, *BABIL* RIP – well, until Daddy Saddam lifts the ban on his son's toy. Meanwhile Uday can play with his other newspaper. (*Babil* does have an online version if you look for it. They even have an English version. Go have a laugh.)

Our leader's generosity has no bounds: since the release of the prisoners, new regulations about almost everything are making us happy Iraqi citizens. Everybody in Iraq can get huge loans to build a house for almost no interest now. And do you have a business which is struggling? Go get a government loan, they only ask for 1/4 of the loan as collateral. Did you fail your exams and did not graduate? That's OK. Daddy Saddam says you can get back to school, even if this is the third year you fail and you would have been chucked out.

But the best is the car gifts everybody (except *me*) is getting. The latest addition to the list of recipients of $30,000 car gifts are judges. Actually, they were cheated. They only got Hyundai 4x4s

----
+ Saddam Hussein's elder son, killed by US troops on 22 July 2003.

that no one has seen before. The police got Maximas and Avalons. I wonder how it feels getting paid $15 a month while driving a $30,000 car?

I suggest the Iraqi police force start practising for a choral version of Squarepusher's 'My Red Hot Car'. OK . . . all together now:

'I'm gonna fuck you with my red hot car . . .' Don't be shy. Download the track. It's brain-twistingly, spine-tinglingly good, really.

Raed, I heard your uncle is travelling to Jordan in the next couple of days. This makes you the lucky winner of a freshly burned music CD. Mainly stuff off Air's *10,000 Hz Legend* album, plus some other things I found at Alan's. If that shop closes I'll die. He even has a special stack just for me. He calls it the 'shit no one but Salam buys'.

:: salam pax 12:16 PM [+] ::

Tuesday, 26 November 2002

My day/night cycle is totally screwed up because of Ramadan. What is supposed to be lunch doesn't take place until 5 p.m. and everybody avoids work until after Iftar – and then stays up really late watching Egyptian soap-operas. Evil_Boss_Creature doesn't understand the necessity of watching *Al-Attar and His Seven Daughters* followed by *Dharma & Greg* at 2 a.m. daily. Just before that, everybody has Suhur (which is the last meal you're allowed to have before dawn – but since no one is going to wake up at 4 a.m., Suhur in this house is at 2.30 a.m.). So, as the Musaharati starts beating his drum (they walk around with drums to wake up people at Suhur time) we go to sleep. Then wake up late for work and spend the day in a foul mood because coffee and tea have been banned until Iftar, which is supposed to be at sunset (around 5 p.m. these days). But because my mother is Shia Muslim and Shia just have to complicate everything, we don't actually eat until 5.30 p.m. You say that half an hour wouldn't make much difference? You're wrong. It makes all the difference in the world. It is the only time I wish my father would be a bit religious and insist on Sunna traditions instead of Shia.

I don't care – just let me eat!

Ya Allah, why can't Muslims even agree on a common time for Iftar? This is trivial, but it becomes essential. Now who was the genius who said 'God is in the detail'? Architects would say it was Mies van der Rohe.+ Others might say Wittgenstein – and Raed, being Raed, would claim he was the genius.

It is not only the time for Iftar that Shia and Sunnis turn into a big deal. There is also the debate about whether to cross your arms or let them dangle by your sides during prayer. Who cares? Just get on with it! And what am I supposed to do if I ever decided to pray? Hang on to my belly with one hand and let the other dangle? But I give one piece of advice: if you were ever cornered and had to choose, go for Shia. Very dramatic. They love ceremonies and during Ashur it is OK for men to cry, wail and generally be drama queens – everyone will consider you very devout.

What both Shia and Sunni Muslims do agree about is that fasting includes abandoning all worldly pleasures. You are not allowed to have a single naughty thought from daybreak until sunset. You can turn it into Sodom and Gomorrah after Iftar as no one would care, but not before. And to help us keep our thoughts clean, most Arabic TV stations start editing out kisses and embraces in movies and shows. The ART network even suspends its two music channels until after Iftar, then it's belly dancers galore. Even the Showtime network ('bringing you the best in world entertainment™' – i.e. recycled American TV) blacks out scenes. First I thought it was a mistake. It isn't. I am not allowed to see the kiss in *Dharma & Greg*'s title sequence in case I have nasty thoughts about Greg.

Ramadan is also the time when everybody remembers the *argila* pipe (Shisha, Narghila or Hookah – but never Hubbly Bubbly). Don't get any ideas, it's not a bong. There are no 'illegal substances' used – I would if I could find any, but alas. Originally the tobacco was mixed with honey, fruit juice and small chunks of fruit to give it flavour. Now you can buy them mixed and artificially flavoured. See The Sacred Narghile.++

+ The architect Ludwig Mies van der Rohe (1886–1969), famous for his dictum 'Less is more.'
++ www.techism.com/narghile.

My cousin, K., is like an *argila* expert. Having got bored with his favourite apple flavour, he decided to improve it by using an apple creatively. Instead of using the normal *argila* head (check the website just mentioned; this guy has photos of all the *argila* parts I am referring), you poke holes in an apple just like the *argila*-head, cover the top with foil and you get an *argila* that tastes very appley. I have a very creative cousin. This totally justifies the five years he spent at the college of engineering. Next time he will make cigarettes out of bananas.

In other local news:

The city of Qurnah in the south of Iraq (way down the map, exactly where the Tigris and Euphrates meet) was bombarded for two days. A friend who works there says that the planes are bombing an empty area very close to the city, the windows of the hotel where he lives are broken. First no one knew why the Americans would bomb an empty area. Later, when they went to look at the craters, they found out that there were telephone lines buried in that area. The governorates of Basra and Maysan are cut off from the rest of Iraq, telephonically speaking, that is.

In Basra the mythical tree of Adam fell down. Just like that. One day it was there for tourists to take pictures, the next it was lying on the ground. This was supposed to be a tree guarded by Allah and had magical divine healing powers and stuff. I guess Allah doesn't care about the offspring of Adam. This was his way of telling us: 'Forget it. You totally disappoint me.'

:: salam pax 9:03 PM [+] ::

Wednesday, 27 November 2002

At 10.10 a.m., inspectors in six of the UN vehicles, trailed by scores of international journalists, reached military-run Graphite Rod Factory, 25 miles southwest of Baghdad. The UN experts disappeared into the sprawling complex without explaining their precise purpose. Reporters were barred.[+]

+ www.abcnews.go.com.

Boy oh boy. There was silence for almost five minutes in the street, before the collective sigh of relief. Actually, I think it was more like 9.30 when the sirens were sounded, not 10. What I heard was that planes were circling the area where the inspectors were doing their thing. But what is more worrying is that not everybody in Baghdad heard the air-raid sirens. I can't remember when they were tested the last time.

FunFact: during the Gulf War and the attacks in later years, the sirens would start screeching about thirty seconds before the first bomb dropped – if at all. They are almost useless. That's why today, when the sirens were sounded, people stood still for a couple of minutes, then went on with their business. If it was for real we would have been creamed within a minute. No time to run to a shelter, it is more fun to stay out and watch. I already have a comfy chair on the roof for that purpose.

Have to run. It is Iftar time and I am starving.

:: **salam pax 5:01 PM [+]** ::

Monday, 2 December 2002

Diana is blogging again. Letter from Gotham is back.

Did you know that 'the greatest of Jewish Babylonian Hakhamim in recent times' was born in Baghdad? Diana has a picture of him on her site. A while ago she promised that she would tell us about this as part of my on-going discovery of Jewish history in Iraq, but she never did. I am sure she has a post about it stashed away somewhere. Give it to me now, Diana. You said you would.

I am happy she's back. And in case you were wondering, yes I am still telling her things I shouldn't.

:: **salam pax 2:09 AM [+]** ::

Tuesday, 3 December 2002

SAUDI ARABIA

> **Modern electro-shock stun weapons are fast becoming the torturer's high-technology tool of choice, Amnesty International said today, as it called for the banning of exports to any country where electro-shock torture has been committed or where torture is persistent, and for an immediate suspension of their use for law enforcement.**
> 'Saudi Arabia Remains a Fertile Ground for Torture with Impunity'**+**

+ This and following extracts are from www.web.amnesty.org.

SYRIA

Although scores of political prisoners were released, dozens of people were arrested on political grounds. Torture continued to be used routinely against political prisoners.

JORDAN

Hundreds of people were arrested for political reasons and there were reports of torture or ill-treatment of detainees by members of the security services. Political prisoners continued to be tried before the State Security Court.

EGYPT

Torture is systematically practised in detention centres throughout Egypt, and victims of torture and their relatives continued to report harassment by security agents.

PALESTINE / ISRAEL

More than 460 Palestinians were killed by Israeli security forces, including 79 children and at least 32 individuals targeted for assassination. Palestinian armed groups killed 187 Israelis, including 154 civilians among them at least 36 children.

IRAQ

THE DOSSIER+

The whole region is a cesspool. Dictatorships are all around the Arab region. Turkey and Iran fare just as bad as the rest of the lot. But the benevolent western eye looks at Iraq only.

+ This is a link to the UK Foreign and Commonwealth Office website: www.fco.gov.uk/Files/kfile/hrdossier.pdf. The dossier is entitled *Saddam Hussein: Crimes and Human Rights Abuses. A report on the human cost of Saddam's policies* (November 2002). It includes chapters on torture; the treatment of women; prison conditions; arbitrary and summary killings; persecution of the Kurds; persecution of the Shia community; harassment of the Opposition outside Iraq; and the occupation of Kuwait. Three Annexes deal with 'Methods of torture'; 'Cost to fellow Muslims of Saddam's actions'; and 'List of attacks with chemical weapons'. The dossier opens with a quotation from Tony Blair's speech to the TUC Conference (10 September 2002): 'Our quarrel is with Saddam, not the Iraqi people. They deserve better. Iraq is a country with a very talented population. We want to welcome it back into the international community. We want the people to be free to live fulfilling lives without the oppression and terror of Saddam.'

Thank you for your keen interest in the human rights situation in my country. Thank you for turning a blind eye for thirty years. Thank you for providing the support for my government to send two million Iraqis to war with Iran and getting them killed. Thank you for not minding the development of chemical weapons by a nutcase when you knew he was a nutcase. Thank you for not minding that members of the Iraqi Communist Party get acid baths (you don't think that this was used for the first time in Kuwait, do you? The Government has been using these baths since the late 1970s). Thank you for ignoring all human rights organizations when it came to the plight of the Iraqi people. Thank you for keeping sanctions which you knew only weakened the people and had no effect on the Government. Thank you for knowing all this and not minding.

For all your efforts I salute you with a hearty FUCK YOU.

There isn't a single bit of information which is not old and has been rehashed by many human rights organizations before. So what makes you so worried about how I manage to live in this shithole now?

Don't read the dossier on Iraq if you are faint-hearted; except if your name is Raed: he has to because I say so.

Not a single line would raise an Iraqi eyebrow. This is how it is and how it has been. Everyone has heard a thousand horror stories; others have witnessed them and still live here. Bite your tongue and move on. Don't ask.

I forgot to thank all the western construction companies who have built the aforementioned prisons. And the Eastern European countries who provided the training.

So now you care? I don't know whether I am angry, sad or scared. You had the reports all the time and you knew. What makes today different than a year ago?

> **No one doubts the barbarism of Saddam Hussein. It dates back to the period when, under a Conservative government, the UK was willing to sell him arms-related equipment and to give him substantial financial credit so that he could afford to make purchases.[+]**

[+] 'Amnesty attacks Iraq for torture dossier', 2 December 2002 (www.guardian.co.uk).

And while you're at it, why don't you pull out the dossier on Syria? Or maybe Turkey? I am sure you are already layouting the Saudi dossier and making it look as nice as the Iraqi dossier – very good layout don't you think so?

:: **salam pax 2:55 AM [+]** ::

Thursday, 5 December 2002

I understand now why Diana doesn't want to have a comments link on her blog. First, I thought that I would only put a link to the Legendary Monkey's post. She basically did what I wanted to do and for a moment I just felt like hiding behind her. Some of these comments did scare me.

But a couple of hours later I decided I do want to shout back. And I am not putting a comments link this time.

Deoxy wrote a fine suggestion in the comments link below: 'Now SHUT THE F—— UP and learn to appreciate us a little!!!'

OK. Let us all have five minutes of silence to do some appreciation.

I appreciate the dropping of tons of bombs on my country.

I appreciate the depleted uranium used in these bombs.

I appreciate the whole policy of dual containment, which kept the region constantly on the boil because it was convenient for the US.

I appreciate the support the US government shows to all the oppressive governments in the region only to dump them after they have done what was needed of them.

I appreciate the US role in the sanctions committee.

I appreciate its effort in making me look for surgical gloves and anaesthetic on the black market, just to get a tooth pulled out – because these supplies are always being vetoed by the sanctions committee.

I appreciate the policies of a country which has spent a lot of time and effort to sustain economic sanctions that punished the Iraqi people, while it had no effect on Saddam and his power base, turning us into hostages in a political deadlock between the Iraqi government and the US government.

I appreciate the role these sanctions had in making a country full of riches so poor.

I appreciate watching my professors having to sell their whole personal libraries to survive, and seeing their books being bought by UN staff who take them home as souvenirs.

I have so much appreciation it is flowing out of my ears.

Back to Deoxy: 'Fuck us, huh? OK, rot under Hussein's rule – we don't have to help you. You are angry as though we OWE it to you – we don't. Be glad we help at all, EVER.'

Honeybunny, no one asked you to friggin' come here. And no one asked for your help. It is your government that has been poking its nose in the region's affairs. Why is it always forgotten that the US government supported the Islamic extremists during the Cold War era as a way to keep Soviet influence at bay? Well, I guess it backfired now, didn't it? Just as the US support to Iraq has backfired.

> In his affidavit, Teicher writes that 'CIA Director [William] Casey personally spearheaded the effort to ensure that Iraq had sufficient military weapons, ammunition and vehicles to avoid losing the Iran–Iraq war.' The United States supplied 'the Iraqis with billions of dollars of credits,' claims Teicher, and offered 'military intelligence and advice to the Iraqis, and by closely monitoring third country arms sales to Iraq made sure that Iraq had the military weaponry required.'[+]

And guess who Reagan sent in 1983 as an emissary to give Saddam all sorts of military advice? Donald Rumsfeld.

What I want to say is don't stick your thingy in places where it doesn't belong. It will get hurt. And I am definitely not asking for your help, your so-called help has already done too much damage so keep out of my backyard, PLEASE!

We give the stand to Lanny now: 'If all your people got gut and stand up who could fuck you up, eh?'

Excuse me, but who do you think is getting broken bottles shoved up their ass? And who is getting his balls electrocuted? Don't you ever call me a whiner. You don't know what it's like to have a mem-

---

[+] From opendemocracy.net: 'No threat from Iraq' (29 November 2002) by Saul Landau.

ber of your family taken away from you because he is suspected of anti-governmental activities – this suspicion being based on a couple of foreign friends he has. You don't know what your life looks like after a family member has been executed because he spoke to the wrong people and expressed an honest opinion. If I may quote Deoxy here: 'SHUT THE F—— UP and learn to appreciate us a little!!!' You stay where you are and let me deal with my shit.

About Mike's question: 'So, what would you do? Come on folks. Instapundit has brought us all here. Lots of people are reading. This is your chance to show everyone just how stupid George Bush is. Let's hear your ideas that make his look so lame in comparison.'

I do believe that you are smart enough to know there is no answer to that question. And as Lynn has said in her comment, we can't go back in time and undo what has already been done. What is coming is inevitable. Everybody seems so entrenched in their positions. Besides, the regime change plan has nothing to do with 9/11 and al-Qaida or the War on Terrorism. These events only brought everything to a head or maybe even delayed that policy, because the US had to deal with Afghanistan first. I quote from an open letter written on 19 February 1998 to William J. Clinton from the Committee for Peace and Security in the Gulf:

> Only a determined *program to change the regime* in Baghdad will bring the Iraqi crisis to a satisfactory conclusion. For years, the United States has tried to remove Saddam by encouraging coups and internal conspiracies. These attempts have all failed. Saddam is more wily, brutal and conspiratorial than any likely conspiracy the United States might mobilize against him. Saddam must be overpowered; he will not be brought down by a *coup d'état*. But Saddam has an Achilles' heel: lacking popular support, he rules by terror. The same brutality which makes it unlikely that any coups or conspiracies can succeed, makes him hated by his own people and the rank and file of his military. Iraq today is ripe for a broad-based insurrection. We must exploit this opportunity.

And you might also like to take a look at the people who signed that open letter. Among them you will find Secretary of Defense Donald Rumsfeld (the same Rumsfeld who in 1983 went to Baghdad to tell Saddam that the US will give his use of chemical weapons in the war against Iran the blind eye), Deputy Secretary of Defense Paul Wolfowitz and Deputy Secretary of State Richard Armitage.

The US moves in mysterious ways. So don't expect any answers to your question.

Today is the last day of Ramadan. And tomorrow is Eid al-Fitr, so happy Eid to all of you. And may peace be upon us all. I am shutting up for the next couple of days.

:: **salam pax 3:40 AM [+]** ::

Tuesday, 17 December 2002

The dollar is going crazy. $1 = 2,280 Iraqi dinars and a very informed opinion (my favourite liquor-store owner, Mr Satan) says that it will probably end at 2,300 dinars for a dollar tonight. Way too much!

It is freezing cold – well, 5°C – and we are back to two hours of black-out every twelve hours. And the office turns into a cool box the moment the electricity goes.

:: **salam 1:29 PM [+]** ::

Pearls of wisdom from my cousin:

There are three things you can do whenever you like in Iraq:
- get seriously ill
- get arrested
- get executed.

It sounds better in Arabic, because it rhymes.

Cheers.

:: **salam 11:07 PM [+]** ::

Wednesday, 18 December 2002

I am really jealous.

The First Persian Top Weblogs Competition.+

+ topweblogs.com/Winners_22.asp.

This blog[+] won the second prize for blog design. It has a picture of an oriental tea glass! Istikan *chai*, dear?[++]

When are we Arabs going to have something like that? And why have Persians taken to blogging more easily than Arabs? Why isn't there a single Arabic weblog? Why? Why? Why?

Raed, dear, you should start one today. I promise I will always raed it.

:: **salam 2:39 AM [+]** ::

By Allah, it works! I can write in Arabic. I don't know what you see, but I am sure if you have an Arabic-enabled OS, you'll see beautiful Arabic letters. RAED, come on, get on with it! We'll do an Arabic blog – and we will even start our own Arabic blogs competition. I will win, of course.

Mmmm, blogger I love you.

:: **salam 2:52 AM [+]** ::

Thursday, 19 December 2002

While we are all wondering about what Bush is to say[+++] about the Iraqi weapons document, Uday is preparing to have another big party celebrating his escape from the failed assassination attempt in 1996.[*]

This year the party at the Furusia Club will feature Nawal El Zoughbi.[**]

:: **salam 11:36 AM [+]** ::

[+] gapp.blogspot.com.

[++] www.mydevweb.com/images/gapp_logo.jpg.

[+++] 'Bush Is Expected to Say Iraq Failed to Meet UN Terms' (18 December 2002) by David E. Sanger with Julia Preston, in the *New York Times* (www.nytimes.com).

[*] In December 1996 the 32-year-old Uday was wounded when he was shot at as he drove through the al-Mansour district of Baghdad.

[**] A female Lebanese singer. See www.3oyoon.com/newal1.htm.

Saturday, 21 December 2002

Dear Raed,

I never answered that angry e-mail you sent when I told you I am deleting the site (which was very unsuccessful – blogspot does not erase the archives). You said I was a coward and never finish what I start. You know me too well.

Yes, I was scared. I thought that the Reuters and Yahoo France articles were enough to create too much attention. I deleted everything too fast to be able to tell whether that was true or not. But that was not the only reason. I was a bit unhappy about how things were going on the weblog.

Just after deleting the weblog, I told Diana that I wish there was another Iraqi blogger. I have done a sort of a mental exercise on how that weblog would be.

To start with it would be in Arabic and discuss as little politics as possible. If cornered, it would be very pro-Palestinian and pro-Saddam – just to be on the safe side. It would also be filled with quotations from the Koran and Hadith or maybe Um Kalthum songs. What I am trying to say is that most 'western' readers wouldn't get it, because it would be so out of their cultural sphere.

This mess I'm in really bothers me. With all my talk of anti-Americanism (is that a word?) I still make references to their culture, their music and their movies. I got whacked for saying 'Fuck you' – I should have said *inachat khawatkum*, but no one would have understood. Just as most Iraqis don't understand most of what is being said by Americans. We would have smiled politely at each other and moved on.

I feel like the embodiment of cultural betrayal. The total sell-out – and this is making me contradict myself all the time.

You remember that evening we spent at the Books@Café, when you laughed at me when I told you that I believe I am the product of a Muslim/ Arabic culture? You reminded me that just two moments ago I was telling you how happy I was watching MTV Germany and shopping for English books at the Virgin Megastore in Beirut.

I am all the arguments we used to have about us being attachments to western culture rolled into one. This is not the dialogue of equals we used to talk about. I keep making references to their – *every-thing* – because I am so swallowed up by it. Look, I have been sending you e-mails in English for the whole of last year! How sad is that?

Shame on me.

You used to anchor me down. All the magazines we used to read: *Arabic Horizons*, *Aqlam* and the rest. Now I just browse thru them. I am back to *Q*, *The Face* and *Wired*: western trash. And don't ask when was the last time I read a book in Arabic – I would be too ashamed to answer. Moreover, I was getting all those scary questions from the people who read the blog: what do I think about the Kurdish situation? Open letters from Diana, which I was really at a loss how to answer.

OK, that's enough. This is as confessional as it gets. Stopping the blog was not about just being scared. I had lost my bearings a bit and needed to re-orient. Don't get mad at me – the things I said in that e-mail are not as mean as they sound. At least I got you to start blogging here. Maybe a certain blogger will believe that I am not a creation of your wild imagination.

And in answer to Eve Tushnet's[+] e-mail to me ('. . . and to ask whether you would prefer that people here not link to you or whether you don't care'), I *do* care about who links to me. I am very honoured by their interest in my weblog and I am very grateful for all the e-mails I got asking if everything was OK. So, as I always answer that question: 'Link me up baby . . . I am a total linkwhore!'

Some more stuff for Raed:

Remember Zaid – the one who e-mailed us a huge photo of his graduation? He wears traditional Arabic dress now (his *dishdasha* does not touch his ankles, because he turned Wahabi or something). He doesn't look the female students he tutors in the face and – get this – he wears eyeliner: black kuhla. Apparently, the Prophet used to do that. He now has bat shit for brains, officially.

+ eve-tushnet.blogspot.com.

I also saw F. the other day. She was so pregnant I didn't recognize her. Sweet as ever. G. was a fool for letting her slip out of his life like he did.

My mom says 'Hi' and asks when is she going to meet Hiba?

:: salam 12:27 PM [+] ::

Sunday, 22 December 2002

The Iraqi 'Opposition Groups' have met and made plans+ for a post-Saddam Iraq.

I feel so much more relaxed now. My future is in good hands. Excuse me while I jump around and celebrate this.

> . . . **According to opposition members, Washington wants the opposition to enhance its credibility without growing too independent, so that the United States controls Iraq's political future, yet has a legitimizing Iraqi partner ready in the wings in case one is needed after any invasion.++**

Man, this is way too funny – the way everyone is so blatant about it. At least try to be a bit discreet. No need for that, eh? Just a bunch of stupid Arabs there. They won't notice the strings moving these puppets.

> **There were American officials on hand to monitor the conference, cajoling its leaders in private to meet the goals set by Washington while ensuring that they did not overstep the American-drawn boundaries.+++**

How can anyone think that this meeting was of any meaning or importance? The whole affair was a mess. The speeches were embarrassing and the fighting over each party's position was even more so (just in case anyone starts having 'Hey, this dude is no way in Baghdad – how can he watch and hear this?' thoughts, I am risk-

----

+ 'Groups Outline Plans for a Post-Hussein Iraq' (18 December 2002) by Craig S. Smith, in the *New York Times* (www.nytimes.com).

++ See above note.

+++ See above note.

ing a hefty $350 fine and possible prison for having satellite TV). Very early on a Kurdistani Sunni group threatened to withdraw from the meeting if Sunni Kurds were not represented at this meeting – but nobody cared because the American organizers of this meeting (headed by Zalmay Khalilzad)✦ had no interest in that bunch of fools.

The result of the four days was a 25 Recommendations document full of hot air dictated by the US. It does say in paragraph two that the groups appreciate or welcome (depends how you want to translate it) the help of the international community for supporting the Iraqi people in helping them end the dictatorial regime and their help in rebuilding Iraq – BUT refuse any political intervention in future Iraqi affairs. I say bullshit. Let's assume they are independent enough to make their own decisions – how do they expect that anyone would give them a free lunch?

'Here, let us send you huge military backing, risk the lives of our people and spend huge amounts of money, just because we like you.'

If you're going to ask for favours, you have to give something in return. And that's a mighty big favour you're asking. But since we know they are not really that independent and everything said in that declaration was approved by their American minders first, that paragraph means nothing, just like the rest of the meeting, speeches and final recommendations.

> . . . **several senior members of some of the largest groups said privately that such statements were largely political posturing, because none of the opposition groups wants to be seen as an American patsy.**

Poor deluded fools. Seen as a patsy? You ARE a patsy!

The only good thing I heard during the four-day charade was this:

> **After pressure from the Constitutional Monarchy Movement (CMM), the plans envisage a referendum on whether the country should**

✦ The Afghan-American Dr Khalilzad was UN special envoy on Iraq and, previously, to Afghanistan.

remain a republic, or restore the monarchy, which was overthrown in 1958.[+]

It is not that I particularly like the Constitutional Monarchy Movement[++] (Raed, do me a favour: check the link and tell me if there is anything worth reading – my access to it is blocked). The CMM and INC (Iraqi National Congress headed by Ahmad Chalabi) are the main puppets in the American game. See this nice photo[+++] of both of them with Under Secretary of State Thomas R. Pickering in 1999 (Chalabi in the middle and king-wannabe Ali bin Sharif Al Hussein on the right). Here is another mugshot of Ali bin Sharif Al Hussein.[*]

In fact, Al Sharif Ali's speech at the meeting was one of the most embar-rassing. He is the best example why I say the Iraqi opposition groups outside Iraq are so out of it. This person who wants to be the head figure of my country can't even speak my language. He stammered and stuttered, pronounced the words as if he had never seen Arabic before. I was wonder-ing whether he was read-ing an English transcription of the Arabic words, because they sounded so wrong. He has never set foot in Iraq. He suddenly got interested in the future of this country in 1993 – no one had ever heard of him or cared about him before that. Anyway, I had a point, this is not it.

I have decided if that referendum ever happens I will vote for a constitutional monarchy. Besides having acquired a lifetime allergy to the word 'president', I think a monarch who doesn't have much say will do less harm than a president who has to fight for his position every couple of years – and once there wouldn't want to leave. This might be wrong, but somehow I think if we did actually reach a point where we have a multi-party system, it will be better to have to deal with ministers and opposition groups rather than a single egomaniac. Oh, I don't know . . . I just don't want to have to say the word 'president' for a while, so give us that wimp from the CMM – better still give us Prince Ra'ad bin Zaid bin Al Sharif Al Hussein. That

----

[+] 'Iraqi exiles plan path to power', (17 December 2002), on the BBC News website (news.bbc.co.uk).

[++] www.iraqcmm.org.

[+++] www.meib.org/images/9911_inc.jpg.

[*] www.meib.org/images/f_hussein_sharif.jpg.

would be good – at least he IS Iraqi and speaks Arabic and has been living in Jordan, not like that Ali who spends his time in decadent western cities.

Wednesday, 25 December 2002

The good news first. We are going to celebrate New Year at my parents' place. They are throwing a party and since the house will be a mess anyway I am occupying the upper floor for my partying purposes. Everyone is invited to bring a friend, a bottle of whatever you drink and a candle. Make that *lots* of candles – the electricity situation is getting out of hand.

The last couple of days you were lucky if you live in an area where the black-out is for five hours a day only. We have been de-electrified for seven hours today and the day is not over yet. Some areas in Baghdad have had ten hours of darkness. And it is not improving. Other governorates are getting half an hour of electricity if at all.

There is an official explanation: maintenance. I say: bullshit. They are probably packing away those generators.

You learn to deal with the scheduled black-outs. You know when they are and for how many hours. But the last couple of days have been really bad – very erratic. They turn it on and off whenever they like. We just freeze and thaw, then freeze again. It has been very cold for the season and it is expected to get colder. The prices of kerosene heaters have gone thru the roof. There is a local factory (state owned), which manufactures these heaters – at 130,000 Iraqi dinars a pop. But buying one requires approval from the general manager. Don't ask. I can't figure why. It wouldn't be called bureaucracy otherwise.

Now take your newly acquired heater and stand in front of the company's building. Someone will offer you 200,000 dinars for it within a minute. Look for it in the shops and you will find it for 260,000 dinars! That's the free-market economy, isn't it? I decided it was cheaper to bring down an extra blanket.

Because of these sudden electricity black-outs, this is the third time I have written this post. I keep forgetting the SAVE button. Not any more – AUTOSAVE came to the rescue, every five minutes.

A couple of days ago the *New York Times* published another article by John F. Burns. Does anyone know if there is a photo of him somewhere, because if I see him on the street I really want to tell him how off-the-mark he can get when he gets carried away. More on that later.

> **The Iraqi currency, the dinar, had gone into free fall, losing 25 per cent of its value against the dollar.**[+]

It has been very weird with the dinar the last couple of weeks. It is floating between 2,200 and 2,300. Yesterday, at night when I went to exchange my hard-earned dinars to $$ it was 2,285 – and the dealer expected it to go up a bit. Many of the wholesale shops at Alshorja and Kifah streets stop buying and selling the moment the dinar starts going crazy, which happens often enough. I went to buy a new monitor for my computer (my old one blew a fuse when the electricity came back with a surge – it made a *zzzzttt-ppfffttt!* sound and died) and the dealer had to check for the price of the dollar before selling me the equivalent of $140 – it is getting to be that silly.

Burns does suggest a reason:

> **. . . somebody high in the Government had dumped dinars on the market to buy tens of millions of dollars in a few hours.**

Very probable, but there is another reason: no one wants to hold on to eventually worthless Iraqi dinars. Prices of real estate and cars have gone up very quickly, almost doubling in very short periods, especially unbuilt land within the Baghdad city limits. Investment loans with lower-than-low interest rates are being ignored. No one wants to have money floating around. And get all of your gold out of the safe deposits as well. Some of you know the meaning of *Farhud* in Arabic. If a bomb hits a bank it will be *farhud*ed . . .

[+] 'In Iraq, Fear and Mumbling at the Top' (22 December 2002) by John F. Burns, in the *New York Times* (www.nytimes.com).

I am straying away from the subject. The point is not only high government officials buying dollars like crazy off the market – everybody else is also doing it.

Talking of money, there is a very pressing question. What are we going to do with all the notes? They all have Saddam's face on them. From the worthless 25-dinar bill to the newly issued 10,000-dinar note?

More from the article:

> Last month, Uday's wings were clipped when the Government suspended his newspaper after it published articles that seemed intended to expose incompetence and corruption in the Government.

It is back in print. Two days ago I walked into the office and found it on my desk – still being printed with the same smudgy, cheap ink. You would think Saddam's son would use good materials.

> If anybody but Saddam Hussein himself seems like the perfect totem for all that is past, it is Uday. Yet his posture now is to present himself as the one Iraqis can turn to, should they want a more modern man to lead them out of the dead-end his father has led them to.

Sorry? What posture? Everyone except his closest 'friends' knows that he is a sick monster. He had already driven himself into a dead-end before his father did. Families walk out quietly when he enters a restaurant, because he is known to send one of his boys to bring him the women sitting at the closest tables to 'join' him. People hate him, as much as they fear his father. So no one is looking for him to lead them anywhere. What a pointless thing to write.

Anyway, since it is the season to be merry, here is a funny little story about Uday.

In the early 1980s the Iraqi Hunting Club had a new indoor swimming pool built. Quite big and state of the art. They decided to have some sort of a party to announce its opening. A nice classy affair. At around eleven, Uday comes in with his entourage, wearing a white tuxedo and top hat – there is still a photo of him in that tux being printed on calendars, but without the top hat. He has a couple of drinks, then decides that the party is boring, so to liven things up a bit he commands everyone to jump into the swimming pool and unleashes his dogs (i.e. bodyguards) to push people into the pool. Has a good laugh and leaves. A fun guy, eh?

:: **salam 1:40 PM [+]** ::

Friday, 27 December 2002

Hmmm, is he ignoring me?

:: **raed 12:23 AM [+]** ::

No-no-no, Wallahi, I'm not ignoring you. I called you on Thursday around 11.30 a.m. – three times. I kept ringing, but you didn't pick up. I know you know it's a call from Baghdad, so why didn't you pick up? I had nothing to do and thought we might chat a bit. I called your brother and talked with him instead.

:: **salam 11:49 PM [+]** ::

Saturday, 28 December 2002

Word of the day: 'de-Saddamization'.

As seen on page 34 of the *Guiding Principles for US Post-Conflict Policy in Iraq* report,[+] published by the Council on Foreign Relations (CFR).[++]

If you don't feel like reading the whole report, just take a look at the last three pages. The 'three-phased approach' the paper suggests is outlined in a chart.

There is another interesting article on that site: 'Reconstruction: A Checklist for Would-be Nation-builders in Baghdad After the Fall of Saddam.'[+++] It gives the gist of that 35-page paper. Some of it sounds like the list my mother would have given my baby-sitter:

[+] www.cfr.org/pdf/Iraq_TF.pdf.

[++] www.cfr.org.

[+++] www.cfr.org/publication.php?id=5288.xml.

Go slow, but steady, on democracy.
Strengthen Ties that Bind.
Mind the neighbours.

:: salam 1:04 PM [+] ::

Sunday, 29 December 2002

A week ago, Jonathan (The Head Heeb)[+] posted a comment on my Letter to Raed specifically about me saying that I feel like I have betrayed my culture. I didn't want to write a response at the time, because I didn't want to start another who? where? what? thing going on. Been there, done that (Hi Al).[++] Hoping that everybody is too busy getting themselves into gear for New Year parties, I thought I could sneak in a response and hope no one notices until it's too late.

You say: 'It's easier to talk to people who share one's background and assumptions, but it's more rewarding to understand the rest of the world and to be understood in turn.'[+++]

Believe me, I know this. I have been rewarded immensely. My life was not only enriched by all that I have been exposed to, but very much transformed. In the comments you wrote 'I want to know about the Egyptian soap operas too. It's selfish of me, but I want to be a guest at the party.'[*] I don't think that's selfish. This is also the reason I read weblogs, even the ones which are very personal. It's a glimpse into a world that I might have not seen before and usually is, as you said, very rewarding.

The feeling of betrayal comes from somewhere else. There was a time when I thought that one of the best things that has happened to me is that I have not been 'rooted' anywhere. I felt that I could feel at home wherever I go. Culture, as in my cultural heritage, was not something I could betray, because it was not part of how I saw myself.

[+] 'The Head Heeb: Knocking Down 4000 Years of Icons': headheeb.blogspot.com.
[++] Al at the Culpepper Log.
[+++] From 'The Head Heeb'.
[*] www.haloscan.com/comments.php?user=jonnaomi&comment=86452382#117.

But this has changed. In this day I am forced to identify myself with something I don't fully believe in. They see a name, a passport and I am lumped with people and things I don't think I belong with. Actually, when I think about it things haven't just changed overnight: I was probably fooling myself or was a good chameleon. So, instead of arguing with whoever, I decided to stop fighting it. It is who I am after all — well, sort of. The problem was that I found out my brain needed some serious re-wiring; I have major blank gaps and disagree with so much. Which leaves me in limbo. This is where the feeling of betrayal comes from. I can't fully connect as much as I try. So if I do understand the lyrics Um Kalthum sings (I see you have used the Egyptian pronunciation 'Kolsoum'), I can't quote the classical poets (whose poems she sings) like my cousins do.

One more thing: thank you, Ikram, for your kind words and under-standing.[+] To use an Americanism: you just, like, totally get it. Thanks. The bit about farsi-blogs is spot on.[++]

:: salam 3:14 PM [+] ::

> **A convoy of anti-war activists, likely to include dozens of British volunteers, will leave London next month to act as human shields protecting strategic sites in Iraq.[+++]**

Oh please, not again.

> **'These people will be distributed to vital and strategic installations in all Iraqi regions,' said Saad Qasim Hammoudi, an official of the ruling Baath party.[*]**

[+] www.haloscan.com/comments.php?user=jonnaomi&comment=86452382#111.

[++] Ikram said: 'Salam's expressed envy for the Perso-blog community. Iranians have created their own space, in Farsi, and do not need to "represent their race". A Farsi blogger can blog about (frex) anime in a wholly Iranian context and not answer questions or even think about how Americans are politically viewing his anime blogging. So, if you accept that this is what Salam wants — why can't he just stop whining and do it? Why not blog in Arabic, write about Egyptian soap operas, and ignore the Americans. Why not create his own "space" where he can be ordinary?'

[+++] '"Human shields" head for Iraq' (29 December 2002) by Paul Harris, in the *Observer*. See www.guardian.co.uk.

[*] 'Iraq turns to human shields' (24 December 2002) by Suzanne Goldenberg, in the *Guardian* (www.guardian.co.uk).

You're just playing into their hands. I would have understood if they were getting humanitarian aid ready – medicine, food, transportable medical care units, anything but being human shields.

'Nobody is naive enough to believe that a superpower like the US is not going to bomb Iraq because there are peace people there,' said Mary Trotochaud.⁺

So why are they coming? Getting killed won't help anyone. If you want to help, be there at the border where a big number of refugees is expected: they will be scared, maybe injured and in need of help. Sitting in a power station hoping that it won't get bombed is silly; we don't have enough power now. I don't care if an already defunct power plant gets bombed. Wait at the border with a small power generator and water treatment equipment – that is real help. Their hearts are in the right place and their support is much appreciated, but their efforts should not be abused. We need you ALIVE.

:: salam 3:17 PM [+] ::

Readying itself for full-scale war, the Iraqi trade minister, Mohammed Mehdi Saleh, said yesterday that everyone in Iraq should have a stockpile of food to last three months.⁺⁺

Panic attack? Well, not really. We have been stockpiling long before the trade minister advised us to do so. Prices of everything storable or used for storage have gone up because of that. Powdered milk doubled, bottled water practically disappeared and the price of a 40-litre plastic barrel has gone up from 5,000 dinars to 12,000 (that I regret not buying a month ago). It is the fact that the trade minister said it which is scary – they are not usually so frank.

:: salam 3:22 PM [+] ::

⁺ See note opposite.
⁺⁺ 'Saddam readies Iraq for total war: civilians stockpile food as army plays wargames' (27 December 2002) by Ewan MacAskill, in the *Guardian* (www.guardian.co.uk).

Well . . . I would like to announce . . . with pleasure . . . the launch of our Arabic 'beta version' release! Thank you, ladies and gentlemen and Salams . . .

:: raed 6:57 AM [+] ::

[salam]: I tell you what, you write whatever you want in Arabic, I will append a translation. *Ahlan ahlan*, made my day.

:: salam 7:02 AM [+] ::

Santa Claus!!

The Iraqi trade minister, Mohammed Mehdi Saleh, announced yesterday that Iraq has signed contracts with French Peugeot and German Volkswagen to buy 10,000 cars for distribution among the Iraqi population.

My suggestion is that we add 2,500 Russian Lada cars; 500,000 Chinese kids' watches; 2,500 SsangYong cars [*Salam: Korean??*]; ten tons of spices from India and ten from Pakistan . . . so who else needs a Christmas present??? And ten tons of coffee from Brazil – we don't want to repeat the fiasco with cars.

[salam]: *Non-Iraqi readers will not get the Brazilian car reference. In the early 1980s the Iraqi State Company for cars imported thousands and thousands of a VW Passat made in Brazil (rumour was that this was part of a clause in an arms deal or something, who knows?). This car was very cheap, it was everybody's second or third car in the house. Your bratty kid wants a car? Buy him a Brazili (which means 'Brazilian'). The problem was it was the worst car you can imagine. Not suited for the heat of the Iraqi summer, it broke down spectacularly. The next batch was a bit better, but still rubbish. Until this day it is the most common and affordable car in Iraq. It is so part of Iraqiness in the 1980s there are songs about it. But it is still rubbish.*

:: raed 7:56 AM [+] ::

Look at this article on the *New York Times* website.✚

If this wasn't so sad it would be beautiful. The electricity went out at the Christmas week concert performed by the Iraqi National Symphony Orchestra. The last time I went was when they were still playing once a month at the Rasheed Theatre. Now they play at the Ribat Hall. Everybody was sad when they were moved out of the Rasheed, because the Ribat is just an abandoned ruin with bad acoustics. They sounded depressing then and I stopped going. The Rasheed Theatre – after the French Cultural Centre stopped using it for performances of French artists and movies – is now rented by a 'commercial' theatre group who prefer silly slapstick comedies.

:: salam 11:50 PM [+] ::

✚ 'In Baghdad, There's Little Romance in Music by Candlelight' (26 December 2002) by Neil MacFarquhar, in the *New York Times*: 'The musicians of the Iraqi National Symphony Orchestra, elegant in black tie or long black skirts, were just settling into their places on the final night of their Christmas week concerts when the electricity failed and the performance hall was plunged into darkness' (www.nytimes.com).

Friday, 3 January 2003

Dear Raed,

I know you probably won't be able to read this today. I hope by the time you will your aunt will be out of the ICU⁺ and in good health. Don't fall apart. Your mom told me you had a fight with H. earlier. Don't do that over the phone. I am sure she loves you and whatever you or she said was because you both are under so much stress considering the circumstances.

I also want to thank you for being so unpredictable and showing up in Baghdad on the 31st. Who knows, this might be the last time we see each other for a while. I am very happy you came. You know, checking around I found out that quite a number of our friends and relatives are having guests from abroad spending their Christmas week off here in Baghdad. Zaid is especially happy with his friend's visit (you know, the one he keeps telling us is his only real friend ever – I guess we were chopped liver). What? Is everybody saying goodbye? It feels like being on the *Titanic* and knowing what will happen to it. So, everybody, just stop hugging and kissing – I won't die, dammit.

:: **salam 10:59 PM [+]** ::

Saturday, 4 January 2003

I always wondered what those leaflets the Americans are dropping in the south of Iraq looked like. A friend of mine told me that the one

----

⁺ Intensive-care unit.

he saw looked in colour and size like a $100 bill (I did read some-where that they dropped leaflets 'printed in green'). Pretty neat. I can imagine people running around snatching them from the sky. Pennies from heaven. I wish I knew someone who lives there well enough to ask him to bring me one.

The latest, umm, droppings (sorry that was cheap) were not that good apparently. CNN.com has one on its site.[+] Take a look. I demand better graphic design. This looks like an ad for kids' radio. I would love it if they would have The Designers Republic[++] as graph-ic consultants. That would make these leaflets true collector's items.

Come on, are you starting an Axis of Bad Taste now?

:: salam 2:00 PM [+] ::

Monday, 6 January 2003

Today wasn't only a holiday (the 82nd anniversary of the Iraqi Armed Forces), but the sunniest day we had for a while. And what do I spend it doing? Ordering and arranging the 'emergency sup-plies' in the storeroom upstairs. Now that the Iraqi trade minister has advised us to stock up, no one is afraid of being accused of being screwy and paranoid.

After spending a couple hours organizing the mess, I think we have too much sugar and too little detergents. Back to the store. Boy, is that shopkeeper making a fortune from the orders he is getting. I wonder if the trade minister only gave that warning to empty their full storehouses? Because if the war doesn't happen, I am dumping all the stuff I bought in front of his house and demand he buys the lot. Pronto.

And in another unprecedented display of care towards the popula-tion, the Government started digging water wells in various residen-tial areas in case of water shortages. In schools, near Party quarters and other controllable places. I am pushing for our own well at the house of Pax, but my father thinks I've gone mad. It's not

----
[+] See www.cnn.com/2002/WORLD/meast/10/28/us.iraq.leaflets/index.html.
[++] www.thedesignersrepublic.com.

expensive and they only drill a hole the size of a CD, thirty metres deep and disco! You've got water. Not for drinking of course, but still it's water. I mean, it's my back they'll break dragging water back from the nearest well. (Actually, I see his point. This *is* paranoid and crazy. Forget the well.)

They have also called on the ration distribution centres to come and collect the rations for May, which means we're getting three months' rations in February. Now I am certain they just want to empty the storehouses.

At around 11 a.m. I took a break to watch the speech. The first broadcast is always at eleven and they repeat it every couple of hours afterwards. It was the usual Saddam-ese:

> **If anyone attempts to intimidate you, the people of Iraq, repel him and tell him that he is a small midget, while we belong to a nation of glorious Faith, a great nation and an ancient people who have, through their civilization, taught the human race as a whole what man was yet to know.**

The President was never a great orator. If you're looking for great, then you have to listen to Mubarak. But this time Saddam didn't even shout at us the scary bits. Just the 'Da-da-da' school of oration. No fire. It makes you wonder. How come we didn't get a dictator who just burns you with the heat of his words? At least make me believe in what you say for the twenty minutes you're on TV. Not even that. *sigh*

And, boy, was it heavily edited. Not bad, camera-transition stuff, but the 'wait-let's-do-that-again' variety. Mid-sentence cuts. It probably doesn't mean anything, but it is distracting.

There was one single inspired moment near the end of the speech. Saddam looks straight at the camera (the rest of the speech he is looking up and down from paper to camera) and says:

> **The enemy ought to remember the terrible end of all empires that committed aggression against our people and nation in the past.**

With long pauses between words. Pure drama. Loved it. '*Al maseer . . . al mashu'um . . . li kul . . . al imbiratoriat . . . alti aatadat ala umatina.*'

OK, so it doesn't make sense and I have no idea what he's talking about. What 'terrible end'? All 'aggressors' have come and gone with plenty of bounty, from Hulagu Khan to the British. But he scared the shit out of me.

:: **salam 11:12 PM [+]** ::

Tuesday, 7 January 2003

I was looking around for a free online poll thingy to ask the following question: 'How soon do you think IT is going to happen?'

A couple of people have been sending me e-mails saying any day now and I should be careful. And I also agreed with the idea that the proverbial shit will hit the proverbial fan around the 3rd or 4th of February – but I have a new theory. I only missed it because the house of Pax is so religiously not 'with it'.

It is Haj season soon. Unless the US government wants a couple of million pilgrims in the KSA (Kingdom of Saudi Arabia) when it starts military action, nothing will happen until after Eid al Adha, which should be around the 12th of February. Besides we have al-ash hur al-hurum now (Muslim readers help me out here), these are three months in which fighting is *Haram* (sinful).

But if Bush were Dr Evil he would go and start a war during Haj and provoke Muslims around the globe into doing something outrageous. Gets out *his* Weapons of Mass Destruction, directs them at Mecca and – Wham, Bam, Bye-Bye Islam! Starting World War Three. But Bush isn't Dr Evil and I am a fruitcake with pictures of giant lemons on his weblog.

Don't you just love Google? Here is the poll. Get those mouse buttons clicking.

Frankie says war. So . . . what do you say?

- First week of February . . . Haj or no Haj, it's going down.
- Second half of February. It's warmer.
- It's not happening till March/April.
- Nah . . . not until next autumn, it's closer to the elections that way.
- What? Are you bloodthirsty? There will be no war.

Cast Vote!

:: **salam 12:40 PM [+]** ::

Sunday, 12 January 2003

Sorrow is never singular. It always comes in multiples.

Raed's aunt has passed away yesterday. She had to undergo two heart operations in four days and has been in intensive care since the beginning of this year. Raed used to joke about the fact that the only person in his family still interested in political action in Jordan was her, the one with the frail heart. I remember her talking of demonstrations and protests during the events in Palestine last January, while the Jordanian government was threatening to use force if the protesters got near the American or Israeli embassies. Everyone in the family would jokingly tell her that if an officer so much as breathed on her, she would come back home with multiple injuries.

Raed, I can't reach you. Your cell phone has been turned off for days and you don't answer e-mails. I wish I could be there with you.

Today a colleague at the office came to our house to tell us his son died of a brain haemorrhage this morning. He is one of the senior engineers. His son is two years younger than me. Because he is not Iraqi, the paperwork involved in getting him out of the country is surreal. How to explain this to a mourning parent is impossible. I stayed with him for a couple of hours, while others were trying to figure out how to get the family to Jordan as fast as possible. The mother understandably doesn't want to stay in Iraq.

There is no appropriate response when someone tells you about the death of a loved one or a family member. I stutter and stumble thru formal responses which mean nothing really.

My heart and thoughts are with you Raed, and your grandmother, who is the strongest among you. If she has held it together through all what the family has been through before so will you.

:: salam 9:40 AM [+] ::

OK, the results are in:

● First week of February . . . Haj or no Haj, it's going down. **(29)**
● Second half of February. It's warmer. **(30)**

- It's not happening till March/April. **(14)**
- Nah . . . not until next autumn, it's closer to the elections that way. **(9)**
- What? Are you bloodthirsty? There will be no war. **(9)**

Well, February it is then. I wish you could have made up your minds which part of February. Hiding under the bed for a whole month without anything happening is not going to be fun.

I still think they will wait until after Haj and Eid. The last plane full of white-clad pilgrims leaving Mecca will be followed by the first plane dropping leaflets saying 'Go for cover – Boom!'

:: salam 11:52 PM [+] ::

All hell broke loose at the Iraqi ISP. The mail server has been disconnected for three days now. I have no idea what is happening. I don't use that e-mail account. I heard a rumour, but I have little trust in the service provider. The server always breaks down. But I got confirmation from someone who actually saw that e-mail.

Three days ago an e-mail was sent to all users. I have not seen it, but the friend who did receive it says that it was urging Iraqis to give information about weapons stored in their homes and not to show any resistance in the event of an attack, not to support the Iraqi government. It was written in Arabic and had an address to send information to. The mail was sent at 00:00 and fifteen minutes later the mail server was shut down, and still is.

I guess all mailboxes are being deleted now. But what are they going to do about the people who did download their mail?

I'm trying to find someone who has the e-mail, but isn't afraid to admit that he still has not deleted it.

UPDATE: Well, the *Washington Post* knows: 'US Government Starts E-Mail Campaign to Key Iraqis'. So does ABC Online: 'US sends Iraqis anti-Saddam e-mails'. The title of the *Washington Post* article is not exactly correct. My friend is not a 'key Iraqi',whatever that means. Anyone who downloaded their mail around 12 got that message.

AUTHORITIES BLOCK E-MAIL SERVICE
Iraqis began to receive the e-mails last week, visitors there said. The state-controlled e-mail service is available only to a small number of Iraqis, mainly government officials, senior public servants, academics and scientists.

That is also not quite correct. All you need is an ID, a phoneline and cash. It's the cash that gets in the way of people getting the e-mail service. And the fact that Iraq is not a very computer-literate land. Importing computers is banned by the sanctions committee. We get smuggled equipment, which is more expensive. The people mentioned in the article get their service for free; that is what should have been said. But while they get it for free we pay an arm and a leg.

Iraqi authorities have blocked the e-mail service access in an apparent attempt to stop the messages from spreading inside the country, visitors said.

Too late for that. The whisper is a buzz already. People are talking. Everyone wants to see what that e-mail was like.

Methinks the Internet service will be axed soon. We'll see. I wonder if the next step in this geeky game is to hack a couple of official Iraqi sites. Future war or what?

If you call the state company responsible for the ISP now they will tell you the server is down for maintenance. I really feel sorry for the network administrators. They are probably having their fried balls for lunch now. What could they have done?

The Internet is available in Iraq but many sites are off limits and all foreign e-mail servers are blocked.⁺

We'll have to talk about that. Reuters people don't know shit about Internet in Iraq. Or maybe we have just been spammed by a bored spammer. Adnan [adnan.org] thinks we have been spammed too.

Maybe, one day we might even measure global tensions by the amount of politically motivated junk mail circulating around.

⁺ www.washingtonpost.com.

Political spamming. Someone should think of a name for that.

:: **salam 12:27 PM [+]** ::

Monday, 13 January 2003

Daman Asset Management has launched a new investment product – *Daman Iraq Opportunity Fund* – with a view to providing investors with the opportunity to participate in the international reintegration and reconstruction of Iraq.[+]

Well, it had to happen.

The fund, with a life of five years and extendable for another five years, is confident of giving out aggressive dividend payout.

So come on, what are you waiting for? And it's safe. The fund will return the investments to the respective investors with bank interest rate.

:: **salam 12:25 PM [+]** ::

Found this on indymedia.org:

**The inspectors came and looked,
And looked, and looked, and looked, and looked.
They looked high and they looked low,
Every place that they could go.
They looked in every hole and crack,
Each drawer and closet, bag and sack.
They found nothing in a trunk – or
Even in my private bunker.
They did not find a single stash
Of weapons of destruction (mass) . . .
And STILL you won't get off my a**!
I've done all that I can do.
The rest, dear Bush, is up to you.
Please don't be angry, don't be sore.
We don't need to have a war.
Let's go back to the good old days
When your dad and Reagan sang my praise.**

+ gulf-news.com.

I was your faithful ally then.
Why can't we be friends again?
I say, let's let this whole thing drop.
(My best regards to your dear Pop.)

:: **salam 1:32 PM [+]** ::

Wednesday, 15 January 2003

Since my cover was blown by Unqualified Offerings,[+] I might as well just give up and tell you what my true mission is: I am here to brainwash you and get you to join the Party.

I am sure you are wondering what Baath means and whether it involves communal ablution ceremonies. The Party's name in Arabic is Hizb al-Baa – here you make a sound as if you were choking – th al-Arabi, which means the Arabic Resurrection Party; as in the resurrection of one united Arab nation, blah blah blah. Nice, innit?

So what are you waiting for? I said JOIN![++]

Don't come looking for me when your enrolment papers come and you get shipped to Damascus not Baghdad. You should have checked whether this is the Iraqi or Syrian Baath before you signed the papers.

:: **salam 8:29 PM [+]** ::

I am so excited about what I heard on the radio this morning, I can't stop smiling. For the first time the Iraqi government acknowledges the fact the population is not a herd of blind sheep.

In a not-so-direct response to the e-mail 'attack' last Friday night and the anti-government radio broadcasts in the south (btw the mail server was brought back online last night, we all got a 200kb text document about new logins and stuff), the Government is airing a public announcement of sorts.

I almost choked on my tea when I heard it during breakfast.

[+] www.highclearing.com/uoarchives/week_2003_01_12.html#004187.

[++] www.baath-party.org.

It is set as a dialogue between two men speaking in Baghdadi dialect. The first asks the other if he has been hearing the news and if he knows 'Shaku? Maku?' ('What's happening?' 'What's not happening?'). In a Q&A format the other one starts 'explaining' the nature of hostile and unfriendly media reporting: how we should not listen to these things because all they want to do is get to you and undermine your confidence; that all we hear is part of a psychological war.

'But what they don't know,' the wise one says, 'is that we are of strong character and these things don't fool us.'

It is quite long. I will have to listen to it again to remember all that was said.

The e-mails, broadcasts and leaflets are not mentioned explicitly, but this clearly is a response to them. What is very remarkable is that it never, not once, mentions Saddam. They use *nahnu* ('us, the people'), *al-wattan* ('the nation') and only once, right at the end, the wise one uses 'leadership'. Very clever. It is propaganda, but it doesn't overload you with the typical Saddam-ese. It really is the best piece of propaganda I have seen them do.

At one point 'the doubter' asks 'the wise one' about war. The answer is evasive. He says it doesn't matter whether matters 'get hotter or cool down', we should not listen to hostile reporting and believe it. Well, I guess this means I am removing the *New York Times* from my bookmarks, then. I am a good citizen, you know.

You can't believe how excited I am about these five or six minutes. They have acknowledged a crisis situation. They have never done that before. And it is not done with speeches directed to politicians abroad, but to the people, in a simple, story-like way. It's a first. I am celebrating this by not clicking any of my news links and watching Iraqi TV only.

Well . . . for the next five hours at least.

Linky stuff:

I have been getting quite a bit of linky-lovin' from something called Sensible Erection.* I get an ACCESS DENIED screen when I try to

----
* www.sensibleerection.com.

open the page. I can only hope the site has chosen me as the sex-iest Bear[+] in the Middle East (link shamelessly stolen from blee bloo blar)[++].

Talking of sites I can't access:
www.milkandcookies.com – nice name, naughty content?
H.E.Y.Y.O.U.I.K.N.O.W.W.H.E.R.E.Y.O.U.L.I.V.E. – Mr site-zapper has you in his sight: ACCESS DENIED.

:: salam 8:43 PM [+] ::

Tuesday, 21 January 2003

Bad, bad weather. Cloudy skies and having to turn the lights on the moment you wake up because the sun just forgot to rise or some-thing. I am grumpy, having only Travis to listen to at the office is not helping my mood either. How these guys manage to make every-thing sound so depressing is amazing.

A quick run-thru how things are in Baghdad the last couple of days.

Electricity: Two hours off every four hours. My cousin is calling this psychological training for harder times. He spends his two hours in total sensory deprivation, as in no radio, no light, no TV. Only candles and the sound of the rain. While I use my nifty 'con-verter', which is basically a car battery I recharge every time we have electricity – good for light and a small TV (for half an hour, oth-erwise I drain the battery too fast) and I am re-reading *The Ticket That Exploded*[+++] for the third time.

Internet: For some reason the ISP does not have uninterrupted power supply for the servers or something, because they also go down with the black-outs. I don't know, but something happens which knocks people off the server in certain areas at a time and does not allow them to log back on until after two hours, which is the scheduled time for a power cut these days. And three more

----
[+] A link to 'So You Want To Be An A-List Bear?' at www.torque.net~bill/alist/abear01.htm.
[++] blee bloo blar BLOG: Fat. Hairy. Gay. Atheist. Radioactive. Liberal. Whiner at johnkusch.com/johnkuschdotcom/blog.
[+++] By William S. Burroughs.

governorates are going to get Internet this week: Tamim, Anbar and Salah al-Deen. Happy porn-surfing to all.

The Dinar: It is still above the 2,100 per US dollar. Last night it was 2,275 Iraqi dinar and demand is increasing because of the people who are going on Haj. The Iraqi National Bank did respond to the fall of the dinar in a wacky way. They started selling a limited amount of dollars per day per Rafidain Bank branch for 2,000 Iraqi dinar. Every morning you would see lines of black-market dollar-dealers line up to get the $1,500 they are allowed to exchange per person, then go and sell it for the inflated price on the market. Made the fat-cat-dollar-dealers richer and did not solve the problem.

The Rations: The way the Ministry of Trade has been heaping rations on people is seriously hurting the price of the goods included in the rations. Many families depend on selling part of the rations to support their income. Wheat is dirt cheap now. You used to be able to exchange one kilo of wheat for seven pieces of bread, but since wheat is so cheap now bakers give you only three breads. This also goes for the powdered milk. And we have been getting really nasty Egyptian soap. I am sure they wouldn't wash their tiled floors with it for fear of corrosion, but I guess it is good enough for Iraqis. Another bad deal made in the name of food for oil, and another well-connected trader bought an apartment in London.

The Jordanian Border: There is now a special area in the Jordanian part of the border-point where they keep 'unwanted Iraqis' until they find a ride back into the country.

Best way to go to Jordan from Iraq (if you are an Iraqi, that is):

> Take a plane – don't use the much more affordable bus. You have a better chance of getting thru the border if they think you have money.

> Book a return ticket, even if you plan on staying (see above).

> If you plan on coming back, use the bus on the trip back and cash in your return ticket.

> Either have a visa to another country or give a believable reason that you can't stay for longer than ten days. A signed paper from your workplace stating that this is a business trip for so-and-so days is good.

Be prepared to wait for a couple of hours in a room with ten other people until the officer is ready to see you.

Good luck.

Alternatively, go to Syria. They still have their borders open to Iraqis – maybe not for long.

The Inspections: Nobody was paying much attention until they decided to go into those houses in the al-Ghazalia district. That got people talking. Documents or no documents, the whole thing is frowned upon. If they do this a couple more times, the disapproval will not only be from 'official sources'. And there also has been talk about the interviews abroad. The idea of taking your family with you if interviewed abroad does not work. 'Define family for me, please. Parents? Siblings? Wife and kids? Aunts, uncles? What?' And the Iraqi government knows this. Pressure can be applied always.

The Weather: Wet and cold. It has been raining a lot and we even had hail. Absolutely no sun.

Raed (He is not in Baghdad, but in case you were wondering why he isn't posting in Arabic): After being the only one who didn't lose it during his aunt's funeral – which, true to our grief-loving ways, was three days for men and seven for women – Raed has come down with a bad flu and has a project final coming up soon too. But at least he started responding to my e-mails.

Me: *sigh* Whoever invented the term 'between partners' is a desperate optimist. I might as well try here:

> **Obedient slave seeks Master. Whip and users' manual come attached. May need some assembly. If interested, e-mail Addy above. I can cook and will wash the dishes too if 'commanded' to do so.**

Oh . . . and I have changed beers. I now drink Sanabul instead of Farida. It is quite unsettling to find a cockroach floating in a bottle of beer you were just about to guzzle down. This is as exciting as my life gets these days.

:: salam 11:56 AM [+] ::

Thursday, 23 January 2003

[raed]: As bad as it gets.

[salam]: Kefak 7ub.[+] Hope you're feeling better. And how is that Final coming along? The phone got cut off the other day, just when I was going to ask you about that. You know I'm a cheap fuck. You get one call every two weeks. Unless you start paying my phone bills, that's all you're going to get.

The latest addition to sites I can't access are all the www.livejournal.com sites. I hope they don't get on to blogspot.[++] Although if they got livejournal, blogger can't be that far away. Cross your fingers.

:: salam 12:04 AM [+] ::

Monday, January 27, 2003

Well, someone has another reason to get to Baghdad:

> 'Onto Baghdad!
> I want 1,000 tiles, half the blue with the pretty medallion in the middle and half with the little hand.
> Onto Baghdad!'[+++]

Teehee. You are most welcome! You would make the poor guy's day asking for 1,000 tiles.

:: salam 11:13 AM [+] ::

Thursday, 30 January 2003

Jack, the newest member in the shut-up-and-say-thank-you club, had this to say in the comments to the post below:

> Think about it. Where are bomb shelters? Duh, in government or large buildings with a GPS co-ordinate on someone's list. I can't

----
[+] 'How are you, dear?'
[++] Salam Pax's site is hosted by blogspot.
[+++] Posted by Diana at www.letterfromgotham.blogspot.com.

believe after reading some of the articles you posted that you don't think your government wouldn't mind using you as a shield. Just stay in your home. You will be much safer. When someone knocks on your door and says 'US Army/Marines', then you can come out. Believe me, your welfare is at the top of our thoughts. Our goal is to help everyone be as free as us. It may sound corny, but it's true. We have always come as liberators. Thousands of young Americans have died over the last 226+ years to help others be free. With all you have to offer, you guys should be as prosperous and peaceful as anywhere else. Who knows? Supposedly the beginnings of man were there. Maybe we'll have a new beginning there to show the rest of the world how it should be.

Dear Jack,

Duh yourself! Since you obviously have not been to Baghdad, you are not an authority on where the bomb shelters are. These shelters, I think around thirty of them, were built during the Iraq–Iran War. Yes, some of them were part of military complexes, but many were built in civilian neighbourhoods. They were built during a time when the Government would give huge loans to people building shelters in their own backyards and bomb shelters became part of the building code for any public building. Jack, that statement is simply not correct.

Has anyone been able to prove that on the night that shelter has been used as a C&C centre, that there was anyone of importance beside the obligatory Party members? Bad intelligence? Shit happens? Well you pooped on me, buddy. Don't expect me to be all Ah!-Great-America-we-love-you. And your government will be pooping on me some more, now how does that make me feel?

I am not taking any of that 'the great liberators – help others to be free'-talk, because I do not believe there is such a thing in politics called altruism. There are no free lunches and no one does *anything* without some personal motives. So if your government is going to go to war, it is not because they are 'helping others to be free', it's because a hundred other reasons and this one just happens to be a nice one to throw to the public. And no, I will not say it's the oil, because it is not *only* oil, although it is a nice little extra thrown in.

I think maybe you should read this article at Perils of Victory (this link came indirectly via Eve Tushnet✛ – she linked to Looking on the Bright Side, which had a link to perils of victory). It starts with a quote from Graham Greene's *The Quiet American*: 'He was incapable of imagining pain or danger to himself as he was incapable of conceiving the pain he might cause others.' It also quotes an Arab ambassador at the UN saying: 'The consequences will not be immediate. You might see GIs distributing chocolates in the streets of Baghdad and being embraced – for three months. And then the opposition to the new colonial power will emerge, and to any other clients being imposed as Iraqi leaders.'✛✛

You just make it sound so easy. You know it's not. But what the hell? After watching the victorious American army march thru the streets of Baghdad, you'll just turn off CNN and look for another show.

Jack, I hope you understand my view. We simply don't trust the motives of your government. And if that government is going to war with Iraq, we are not naive to think that they are doing it because they want to spread love and freedom. I am not even sure peace and freedom are going to be among the side-effects of this war.

Was just looking thru the comments. Russil, I am quoting you here: 'But Americans shouldn't say that they're going to war for humanitarian reasons. As you can see, it just pisses people off.'

Thank you. I have always been told to get to the point and not go around in circles. That was my point.

:: salam 4:55 PM [+] ::

Everybody got an e-mail from the Iraqi ISP saying that e-mail and Internet services will be irregular and may be cut off for long periods in the next 48 hours.

'Maintenance and improvement of the service' – maybe that should be translated to 'screwing the firewall bolts a bit tighter' or maybe

----
✛ eve-tushnet.blogspot.com ('Conservatism reborn in twisted sisterhood').
✛✛ Diana, remember when I wrote to you about that Sophia Loren movie with that scene? Look, Mr Arab ambassador has seen that film too. This above all things is an image which irrationally annoys me. You told me I was not making sense (I wasn't), but it still bugs me. Is there a way to at least tell them not to distribute Hershey bars or anything with marshmallow filling? SP

they are just dealing with that weird SQL-Slammer-virus-thingy. Uday's newspaper wrote about it today on the last page. Either way, it makes posting a test of patience.

I don't watch enough TV. Just so that no one tells me I have been hurting the Iraqi average TV time, I spent a lot of the last two days watching Iraqi channels. Great entertainment. You see, Saddam, in order to prove that he is A-OK, is almost daily on TV. He gets a number of officers and asks them questions, which he answers himself. He actually said that the West probably thinks that he can't sleep at night these days and has to take sleeping pills. Well you are wrong. He sleeps every night very well, because he knows his people 'are pleased and happy'. Well, that explains the feeling I have. So, no sleeping pills for Saddam – maybe he can give me his. And to prove how relaxed he is, he serves the officers tea, coffee and sweets and drinks it with them (*gasp*). Of course, the coffee sits waiting until he says something like 'Well, drink your coffee, men. No one likes cold coffee.' And as if pre-rehearsed they all lift the small cups and take a sip in one single synchronized move. It looked hilarious.

There is also a programme called *Humat al watan* (*Guardians of the Nation*), which used to be only once a week. Now it's every day around 7.30. It's the official Ministry of Defence programme and between announcements, to draft reservists or such, we get little sketches about evil, evil western governments. (They are not shown on the Iraq Satellite Channel, so you can't see them. But you can watch the daily Saddam hour.)

Latest reservist news? Well, if you were born between 1951 and 1958 you are officially off the hook. No more military service for you boys. And the guys who draw the short straw are 1966–1971. You're up next. This is probably the worst time to do your reservist training. The possibility of paying your way out of the two months is cancelled out because Qusay✦ himself is overseeing the training of the reserves.

✦ Saddam Hussein's younger son, killed by US troops on 22 July 2003.

In the meantime:

Me and the girl from Gotham,**+** we be playin' Blogger Ping-Pong.

She has got some.
You ain't got none.

:: **salam 4:57 PM [+]** ::

Friday, 31 January 2003

A car ride to al-Mansour to get sandwiches, late at night.

Ten new sandbag-protected trenches seen on the way. Appetite totally ruined by thoughts of who will use them and what will happen along these roads.

Maybe exploration journey tomorrow to see what else is being done to Baghdad.

I am either angry or scared. I can't make up my mind.

:: **salam 4:16 AM [+]** ::

I knew it. They did something to the firewall.

Blogger is accessible, but I get a YOUR ACCESS HAS BEEN DENIED message for all the blogspot sites.

Time to take a break and maybe look for a new blog home. Diana will know if I'll post again somewhere else.

Thank you, ladies and gentlemen. You have been a wonderful audience.

Goodnight.

:: **salam 4:07 PM [+]** ::

+ Diana, at www.letterfromgotham.blogspot.com.

Wednesday, 5 February 2003

> **Players and spectators in the arena**
> **Baffled by our moves and by the world's**
> **We are playthings in the hands of time**
> **Dancing to music that is not our own.**

Khalilullah Khalili, Afghan poet[+]

Reader 'anya o' sent me those lines.

There are not enough words to express my thanks for all of you. For your kind words, your concern and the help offered.

Diana, having used the words 'blogson' and 'Salam' in the same sentence, gets to suffer thru all the embarrassing things 'blogsons' do: me going on and on about pointless things and frightening her with the thought of me singing 'Thank You for the Music' wearing my best ABBA costume. Thank you.

Jim Henley, man you are fast. And he knows I just have to tell Diana, so he sends the e-mail to her as well. Thank you. Saying that I have been flattered by your offer is an understatement. Thanks for thinking of me.

Kathy, thanks for all the tips and for offering me a blog home. And thank 'MommaBear' for me as well.

Al, being the first to throw the he's-a-CIA-stooge thing at me will

----

[+] Khalilullah Khalili (1907–1987). See *Quatrains of Khalilullah Khalili*, published by The Octagon Press.

always give you a special place in my heart. This time he wrote me a poem.

Take it away, Al:

Splendor in the Grass

Our ol' buddy Salam, he's a dirty lil' perv
Hussein just can't stop him
Bushy's chances are slim
When he's on a love mission, you know he won't swerve

So our bombs start to droppin' on his city so dear
And the Casbah starts rockin'
While the town folk be gawkin'
In shock as the smoke starts to clear

As the neighbors start looking for their goats most preferred
Past Saddam's charcoaled ass
Follow the bleats in the grass
And find Salam out humpin' the herd.[+]

You owe me a new keyboard. My brother spilled his sugary tea on it after he read this. Now it's all sticky. Thanks, Al.

The lady who calls herself 'a reader': thank you, I hope you keep coming and keeping an eye on me.

Emily (I think hawkgirl.blogspot.com), thanks for offering to host my blog.

And finally, Jason [shellen.com] from Pyra Labs. I was setting up a blog somewhere else when I got his e-mail. I guess this means I will have to tattoo 'Blogger 4 Ever' on my arm now.

I didn't post the last couple of days, because I wanted to see if they were going to block blogger.com as well. If they did that, they would have figured out what this is. But since they didn't, it means they are giving blogspot the geocities treatment. Since the first day the Internet was offered to the public, anything on geocities has been blocked, then later MSN communities, Yahoo groups, anything on Tripod and AOL were blocked. The latest additions are livejournal and blogspot. But what happens is that sometimes, when you are hopping from link to link, a geocities site opens. Press 'refresh' and

----
[+] www.morethings.com/log/.

it disappears. Go back and get to the site from the link that let you see the site and it loads again. I have no idea why this is, but blogspot is the same now. Not that I care. Having had a thousand suggestions from you e-mailed to me and a tetchy brother, I am now set up with two nifty programs which let me go anywhere I want.

This isn't a state secret. Everybody here who wants to use Yahoo or MSN messengers has looked for things which let you circumvent the proxy, but it's a cat-and-mouse game. If they know which sites you're using, they block it and you look for another.

Thank you for making the last couple of months just great. For taking the time to read this weblog, to link, write an e-mail or comment. Most of you know more about what I feel and think than my family does. For starters, none of them know I blog. You do. And Diana just knows way too much for my own good :)

Thank you.

:: **salam 3:26 PM [+]** ::

Powell's speech is around 6 p.m. in Baghdad.✛ The whole family is getting together for tea and dates-pastry to watch the Powell Rocks the UN Show. Not on Iraqi TV, of course. We have decided to put up the satellite dish to watch it. Yes, we will put it away afterwards until the next event. I don't exactly like the thought of two months in prison just to have 24-hour BBC (no free CNN on ArabSat, which is the only sat we get with our tiny dish).

A quick run-thru what is going on in Baghdad before uncles and aunts flood the house. The juiciest bit of news actually happened about a week ago, but I was only told about it today. A couple of days ago it was rumoured that all top officials had their phone numbers changed. Well, who cares? It's not like I call Saddam every night to chat. But today a friend explained why. Around six days ago

----
✛ The US Secretary of State, Colin Powell, gave a dramatic 75-minute speech to the UN Security Council. He presented declassified satellite images and communications intercepts of what were purported to be conversations between Iraqi commanders. He also drew links between al-Qaida and Iraq and held up a vial that, he said, could contain anthrax. Jack Straw, the British Foreign Secretary, praised Mr Powell for having made a 'most powerful and authoritative case', but France, Germany and Russia continued to insist that UN weapons inspectors in Iraq should be given more time.

the phonelines of the Iraqi air defence units were 'attacked'. When you picked up the phone in some of the command units, you didn't get a dialling tone, but a male voice speaking in broken Arabic. What it said is close to what the infamous e-mail said: 'Don't use chemical or biological weapons!', 'Don't offer resistance!' and 'Don't obey commands to attack civilian areas!' and so on. This went on for a couple of hours. Now everyone has new numbers. I have no idea how this is at all possible. I do know that for some rural areas we use microwave signals for phone connections, but they can't be so stupid as to use it for military purposes.

Way to go, Uncle Sam! This is going to make one hell of a James Bond movie.

The trenches and sandbag mountains I wrote about last week are now all over Baghdad. They are not being put there by the army. They are part of the Party's preparations for an insurgence. Each day a different area of Baghdad goes thru the motions. Party members spread in the streets of that area, build the trenches, sit in them polishing their Kalashnikovs and drink tea. The annoyance-factor of these training days depends on the zeal of the Party members in that area. Until now the worst was in 14th of Ramadan Street: they stopped cars, searched them and asked for ID and military cards. Good thing I wasn't going thru that street. I still have not stamped my military papers to show that I have done my reserves training.

Saddam is still meeting officers daily and we have the pleasure of watching these meetings three times every day. Each batch he meets leaves the place with a 1.5 million Iraqi dinars cheque and a brand new car. The latest cars to be put in the warehouses I pass by are Toyota Corollas – all white. The warehouse has around 150 of them (we counted the trucks standing outside). It is said that there are a couple of thousand more new cars waiting just outside Baghdad, parked so close together when one of them caught fire they couldn't get to it fast enough and 38 cars burned.

Don't you just love gossip?

A work-related trip to Arbil in the north of Iraq had to be cancelled when I found out that if I am going to sit in the same car as a WHO staff member I have to get a travel permit from the Ministry of

Foreign Affairs, even if it was 'local staff' (i.e. an Iraqi citizen). The permit takes around three days to issue, which would have made the whole trip pointless. I really wanted to go. There is no border as such, but you go thru an 'Iraqi' check-point, then a 'Kurdish' one, and the best way to get thru them without hassle is to travel in an international agency car – but that requires a permit from the Iraqis. Bummer.

Door bells are ringing – have to go now.

:: salam 5:10 PM [+] ::

Saturday, 8 February 2003

8 February 1963
President Abdul-Kareem Qasim is ousted in a coup led by the Arab Socialist Resurrection Party (the first Baathist 'revolution', later to be called the 'fair maiden' of all revolutions). Abdul-Salam Arif becomes President and kicks out the Baathists ten months after they put him in the President's seat. Saddam is among the group who attacked Abdul-Kareem's car in al-Rasheed Street.

17 July 1968
The second Baathist-led coup. Arif is ousted. General Ahmad Hassan Al-bakir becomes president. Saddam Hussein is vice-president.

16 July 1979
Al-Bakir 'resigns' and Saddam Hussein becomes the President of the Republic of Iraq.

We get a public holiday to contemplate how could there have ever been people who were fooled by Baathist ideology.

One Arab nation with an eternal message!

Unity (*wahda*)

Freedom (*huria*)

Socialism (*ishtirakia*)

Sometimes, when talking to someone who was there during all this – the generation which had a chance to go out in the streets and effect change – it just slips out:

[salam pax]: You were tricked and used, you realize this?
[parental-unit]: Yes, now what? Do you want an official apology?
[salam pax]: No, just wanted to make sure you acknowledge it.

Only my Commie uncle starts shouting abuse at me. :-)

:: **salam 3:49 PM [+]** ::

Lisha has magnetic poetry just for me.+

You know I love this. You should check all her magnetic poems.

Boy, did I miss you – and your site was going crazy the last couple of weeks. Hope everything got sorted out. Sorry to hear you have lost your novel notes.

:: **salam 8:26 PM [+]** ::

Campaign Against Sanctions on Iraq (CASI) press release, dated 7 January 2003:

> **A 'strictly confidential' UN document, written to assist with UN contingency planning in the event of war with Iraq, predicts high civilian injuries, an extension of the existing nutritional crisis, and 'the outbreak of diseases in epidemic if not pandemic proportions'.**

The document is entitled 'Likely Humanitarian Scenarios' and was apparently mentioned for the first time in this *Times* article (23 December 2002):

> **The United Nations is making secret contingency plans for a war that would halt all Iraqi oil production, 'seriously degrade' the country's electricity system, provoke civil unrest and create 900,000 refugees.**

CASI says that it has obtained a draft of this document through a UN source, who has authorized the publication of parts of it.++ With all the talk about human shields and anti-war protests, none of the 'human shields' is thinking of a Plan 'B'. And from what little I have heard, most international agencies, including UNHCR,+++ are say-

----
+ www.vaspider.surreally.net/suddennothing.
++ 'Likely Humanitarian Scenarios', 10 December 2002 (casi.org.uk).
+++ The United Nations High Commission for Refugees (www.unhcr.ch).

ing they are not really prepared or don't have enough funds in case of a 'humanitarian emergency' in Iraq, and even if the funds were available, getting the goods to where they are needed is also a problem. It makes pretty grim reading.

There is one term I have not seen before: Internally Displaced Persons (IDPs). The report estimates the number of IDPs at two million. Refugees to bordering countries at around 900,000 to Iran and 50,000 to Saudi Arabia – they would be 'from Baghdad and the Centre Governorates' (Paragraph 17). I guess the western desert makes Jordan and Syria a bit too difficult to reach, but Turkey would probably also see a lot of refugees (well, they have prepared their tents within the Iraqi border there anyway). A more recent article on the UNHCR site says that the expected number of refugees is around 600,000:

> **The United Nations High Commissioner for Refugees, Ruud Lubbers, said Tuesday between 500,000 and 600,000 Iraqis are likely to become refugees in a US-led military action in Iraq. Lubbers told a news conference in Geneva that half of the Iraqi refugees are expected to flee to Iran while the other half are likely to head to Turkey in the north.**

Makes more sense than going to Saudi Arabia. But there is one little fact that the UN document mentioned above does not state. This is from the UNHCR:

> **Lubbers said a military conflict in Iraq will also produce a large number of internally displaced people in Iraq fleeing the war but, as in the case of the war in Afghanistan, these people would not be covered by UNHCR since they are not classified as refugees under international law.**

So what happens to the two million IDPs?

Back to 'Likely Humanitarian Scenarios'. The report summarizes the scenarios by splitting them into two stages: Emergency and Protracted Humanitarian Requirements. Here is the list for emergency requirements:

- Bridging, material handling and transport.
- Food and necessities for some 5.4 million people.
- Health supplies to treat injuries for approximately 100,000.
- Health supplies to treat the highly vulnerable for up to 1.23 million.

- Health supplies to cater for the on-going needs of 5.4 million.
- Nutrition supplies for 0.54 million.
- Water treatment equipment for 5.4 million.
- Chemicals and consumables for 5.4 million.
- Sanitation materials and chemicals.
- Total range of services for two million IDPs, some of whom may well become refugees. The number that may eventually be in this category cannot be assessed with any confidence.
- Emergency shelter for 1.4 million.
- Family reunion facilities for unaccompanied minors.
- Facilities for 100,000 Iraqi refugees in neighbouring countries.
- Mine Action activities, (de-mining, UXO clearance, mine awareness).

You notice it doesn't make any mention of a possible doomsday scenario if one of the sides uses 'unconventional' weapons. I guess if that happens it would be out of everybody's control. Rather not think about it.

:: salam 11:06 PM [+] ::

Tuesday, 11 February 2003

Very bad Internet connection the last two days. The local servers ping, but no pages load, then suddenly for ten minutes all is super-fine, but I can barely check my e-mails let alone read any news before it goes again. Am writing this just because it became a bit of a habit. We'll see if I post it.

Remember the time just before the Gulf War when everybody was rushing around and people were doing their perfunctory 'Well, we tried, but . . . blah blah blah' speeches? This is what it looks like now. This is 'the re-run of a bad movie' Bush was talking about in one of his speeches. Believe me, I don't want to sit thru it either. Watching the world get in line after yet another Bush and his magic flute.

(Unrelated FunFact: You know the band BUSH? DJs on the English-language radio station in Baghdad (voice of youth) are not allowed to say the name of the band. They have to spell it: 'Bee yu ess etch have yet another single out.' I bet all the DJs there thank

God there isn't a band called Schwartzkopf – imagine having to spell that every time you play a song.)

(Another unrelated FunFact: Do you remember this childish joke? There is a mosaic of Bush senior on the entrance to al-Rasheed Hotel: all visitors have to step on it if they want to get in. Al-Rasheed is where all international state visitors are accommodated. I have seen funny Ministry-of-Silly-walks-like attempts to not step on it. It's silly really. Well, you can't see it any more. They have put a huge rug over it.)

The Adha Eid is tomorrow. Haj is over and time will be ticking out. The streets are full of people buying Eid treats for kids and preparing for the Eid feast. My parents, because they are from two different environments, have separate traditions for Eid. I get to choose where to go for the big lunch, which should be after the Eid prayer in the mosque, but since I don't do that I get a couple of extra hours of sleep.

I will most probably spend the first day with my mother's family. Tastier food: our favourite caterer, Abu-Karam, is making the stuffed lamb and he will, as always, drop by to see how well his lamb has been received and have a drink with my uncles. Besides, around thirty people and four generations make a good party. Big family gathering food fest. Yay.

The war will just have to wait.

Thanks for all the advice on how to get my well water treated. Now I don't need to worry about that any more. What still worries me is the air-tight room business. As much as I try not to think about it, Alan (who started the issue in the comments link) is right. So I guess I have to thank you for offering all the information.

It's just not that easy getting the family to listen. It took me a week to convince them that we needed a well. There is one place where I got even more information from: Imshin had posted something a while ago about that issue, so I went back to check, only to find an even more informative post with a very useful link.✦ (OK, so I am not sure how the proprietors of that site will react if they know an Iraqi is finding their information very useful.)

✦ www.imshin.blogspot.com. Imshin is a blogger from Israel.

Imshin, I hope you and your family will be safe. These days I keep thinking of the lines anya sent me earlier:

We are playthings in the hands of time
Dancing to music that is not our own.

I have so little control over my life these days, let alone understanding where the world is heading to. I hope we will all be spared any unnecessary grief.

Saddam has a new photo taken with his sons on the 4th of this month. Notice the friendly looking pistol in Uday's belt. A perfect family photo.

:: salam 1:34 AM [+] ::

Friday, 14 February 2003

I wasn't going to blog until after Eid, but there is this whole 'authenticity' thing going on concerning this blog.

The people who have been reading this blog for a while know that we have been there and done that (the link is old: Al of the Culpepper Log and I are super cool now – he smacks my butt whenever I do something stupid) and I don't really want to go into it again.

To the people coming from www.wired.com, please always remember that I am no authority on anything. Quoting me like the journalist did there makes me a bit nervous: Salam says this, Salam says that . . . Big media scares me. Trouble is never far away. I hope the article is not part of the print edition – that *would* scare me.

And I am just super-grumpy and will regret this post later.

:: salam 4:23 AM [+] ::

Sunday, 16 February 2003

A first on this blog – here comes a quote from the Koran: '*qulna ya nar kuni bardan wa salamen ala ibrahim*' ('We said, "O Fire! be thou cool and (a means of) safety for Abraham!"') Surah 21. The Prophets.

Plot background: Abraham/Ibrahim and the Heretics are having their equivalent of a WWF smackdown (smashing of idols, miracle face-off, the works). Finally, the Heretics decide to throw Abraham into the fire and tell him: 'Let your God help you out of this!' Thus the *nar* ('fire') is turned into *bardan wa salamen* ('coolness and safety') and Abraham walks out safe and unscathed.

I think I heard that *bardan wa salamen* quote a thousand times during the last four days. People want to believe that what happened in the Security Council will actually shoo away the ghost of war. I don't think it will. The Blix and Baradei reports are as wishy-washy as the first reports. We can quote the parts that say we're co-operating and the 'others' can quote phrases that say the exact opposite. Besides, at this moment I think it is not only about the issue of Iraq and WMDs. It's beginning to look like a showdown between the US of A and the rest of the world. We get to be the example.

Anyway, to watch the Security Council this time you didn't need to sneak up the satellite dish – just find one of the 4,000 Iraqis who have subscribed to the fourteen state-approved sat channels. The Syrian Sat Channel was transmitting the session live, with translation. Most people listened to it on Radio Monte Carlo, if at all.

Actually, most of the people in Baghdad were stuck in the streets waiting for any kind of public transport. This is the first sign of a big organized demonstration. All buses – state and privately run lines – are grouped in various spots in the city to transport the 'demonstrators' from their work places to where the show is supposed to take place.

Drop them at point 'A' and pick them up at point 'B'. School kids would just disappear between these two points – there are a couple of excellent ice-cream places in al-Mansour where one of the 'demonstrations' took place.

This is what it looks like when you are in one of these affairs. You get out of the bus and wait for a mind-numbing couple of hours until they tell you to march. You start walking until you see the guy in the front of your group (usually an eager Party member) start jumping and trying to pump some life into the bored group of people behind him. You shout the obligatory things, pass the stand where the officials and press are waiting, then you get back to whatever you were discussing with the person next to you.

The worst experience with 'demonstrations' people ever had was sometime during the 1980s. I can't remember when exactly, but the Grand Festival Square (*sahat al ihtifalat*), the one with the two intersecting swords, had just been opened a short time before and this was the first BIG demonstration there. It was mainly high-school and university students. Instead of the drop here, pick up there strategy, they decided that everyone should just wait within the boundaries of the square. Guards were all over the perimeter – no one could leave. Then they decided to wait. This was during the summer. By noon kids started dropping and fainting. No water and no food and not even a place to sit in the shade. When they realized it was getting serious they brought in trucks with bread and water tanks. You can imagine what it would look like with thousands of hungry and thirsty kids. Total chaos. No one died, but many were seriously injured and they never did that again. Demonstrations? No thanks. I have mastered the art of sneaking past the green-clad guards.

Instead of getting trapped in one of the streets they have closed for the demos, I stayed home and helped my mother pack things. We have not decided to leave Baghdad if 'it' happens, but just in case we absolutely have to. We are very efficient packers, me and my mom. The worst packers are the emotional ones. The oh-let's-remember-when-I-bought-this-thing packers. We just do it in cold blood. We have done this quite often. We are serial packers. Grrrrrrr.

It's not only us who are packing.

G. (the one who reads novels in atmospherically correct conditions) is helping most of his foreign friends to pack as well. We have said our goodbyes to most of them. The French Cultural Centre stopped all language courses being taught by French staff and they have said their goodbyes and good wishes to their students. The Russians are locating all 2,000 citizens and telling them to leave. (What are 2,000 Russians doing in Iraq anyway?) The Chinese embassy, which is as big as a small village, is empty. If you have read that UN report about humanitarian scenarios, you might have come across something the report calls Phase V. From what I understand, Phase V is something like 'extreme crisis, get the heck out of there' sort of thing. At the moment, UN staff who would not evacuate until Phase IV are being told to take long vacations starting with Eid. Notice 'vacation' and not 'this is officially a Phase IV situation, grab your bags and run'.

Now, the thing Wired.com wrote about – not the e-mails, but the site-blocking and 8e6 Technologies. I know I should not bite the bait, but I can't help it. My guess is that 8e6 Technologies didn't know it was selling the software to an Iraqi entity. It was most probably done by the French, who did the Internet set-up in the first place. Because I was getting a bit worried about who is reading what, I also did a bit of prodding to find out how they decide what to block and what not and it turns out it *is* the mess I always knew it is.

Q: Google gets blocked for days at a time, why?

A: The Mukhabarat minder at the ISP decides that he does not want to bother with doing his daily random checks and just registers the Google URL as blocked. It takes a couple of days and some paper shuffling until someone explains to him that it is not Google that is the baddy and that things can be looked for in other places. The firewall blocks URLs and terms within a URL or search request, but that only works with the popular search engines. The rest is done with random checks of URL requests going thru the servers.

Q: Blocked Arabic sites are more than obviously 'hostile' English-language sites?

A: There are no special requirements concerning languages for the minder to work there.

Q: They do know their porn sites well.

A: Well, it is more interesting to check on them than the politics stuff. Who wants to read when you can look?

Q: Is there a proxy that is not firewalled?

A: Of course: Uday's (i.e. the Ministry of Youth/Olympic committee).

Q: Can I get a username/password?

A: Go fuck a cow . . .

(Well, it didn't hurt to ask.)

Did you know David Bowie says 'God is an American' near the end of 'I'm Afraid of Americans'?

I mean, if Bowie says it, he must know something. He has *connections*, so I'm told.

:: **salam 3:45 AM [+]** ::

Wednesday, 19 February 2003

I am getting a real kick out of posting this:

THE GUARDIAN IS WRONG. Check your sources, baby. In the article entitled 'Iraqi Defence Minister under house arrest', it says:

> **He [Lieutenant-General Sultan Hashim Ahmad al-Jabburi Tai, Minister of Defence] is not only a member of President Saddam's inner circle, but also a close relative by marriage. His daughter is married to Qusay Hussein, the dictator's 36-year-old younger son – considered by many as his heir apparent.**

Wrong! *Falsch! Khata'a!* Qusay's wife is the daughter of Maher abdul-Rasheed, who is a very important military man. He led the armies which 'liberated' the Fao area in the south of Iraq in April 1988. He was put under house arrest a year after that for some reason or other and is now living in the Iraqi western desert raising camels and staying out of politics. Qusay does not have a second wife, only Saddam has. So there is no use saying that those loony Muslims have more than one wife, so maybe she is the second missus Q. Hussein.

> **Last night one independent source in Baghdad contacted by the *Guardian* confirmed that Gen. Sultan was in custody. 'He continues to attend cabinet meetings and appear on Iraqi TV, so that everything seems normal,' said the source, a high-ranking official with connections to Iraq's ruling Baath party. 'But in reality his house and family are surrounded by Saddam's personal guards. They are there so he can't flee.'**

I – not a 'high-ranking official' – can tell you that his family is not under house arrest. His son is still driving that fancy car around Arasat Street, intimidating everybody like all good sons of ministers do.

I first heard this on the BBC World Service this morning and then my father told me he read it on the *Guardian* website. I thought I should share it. Now excuse me, I have to get back to practising my funky-chicken moves.

:: salam 2:05 AM [+] ::

Back to Iraq 2.0[+]

I just can't remember how I stumbled into this weblog, but today reading it was like having my ears tickled from the inside (you know, like that guy on the MTV station break). Listen:

> **By not supporting a democratic Iraq, by appointing con-man and a flim-flam artist Ahmad Chalabi as provisional leader, by inviting Turks to occupy Iraqi Kurdistan and promoting some gauzy ill-thought-out vision of a democratic Middle East imposed by force of arms, the Big Idea idealism, which never rested comfortably on the shoulders of a president who detests complexity, comes off as callow, cynical and . . . what are the words? Oh, yes: 'Absolute bullshit.' The ideas and principles upon which the United States was founded – 'liberty', 'freedom', 'justice for all' – and for which we allegedly fought and won two world wars and the Cold War, have become mere words, talking points and awkwardly mouthed slogans used to make a case for a war that no one except for a small junta in Washington wants.**

Is he good or what? Check out the link. Do you see that photograph on the top of that article? This shop, Mazi, is like a legend here in the central governorates. 'It's, like, this huge supermarket where you can buy *everything*.' Baghdad doesn't have supermarkets, only corner-store kind of shops. Every Iraqi who gets to Duhok (they are not many, since it's like going into another country) has to keep telling you about it for hours. It's a supermarket, for Allah's sake – and a pretty expensive one at that. Keep your cool. But I don't mind the presents they get me from there.

:: salam 1:37 PM [+] ::

[+] www.back-to-iraq.com.

Friday, 21 February 2003

These are the days of crazy weather, very colourful. We had rainy-clouds-grey two days ago, sunny-bright-yellow the day after and desert-sand-red the day after that. But it is warmer generally and the nights are beautiful with a bright moon when you can see it thru the clouds or sand. The moon has started waning now and getting closer to that scary 'dark of the moon' phase. Most people think that if anything is going to happen this month, it will start during the darkest nights. We'll see.

In Baghdad and other cities in Iraq people are busy welcoming the Hajis back from their trip. Cars with green and white flags drive the new Hajis around the city and their houses have the same flags on them. The people who went to Mecca in coaches take quite some time to get back to Baghdad. The funny thing is that even the people who travelled in airplanes are only arriving now. Some of them slept for three nights in airports until they got their chartered flights – and the Saudi government would rather have the Iraqis in the airports than roaming about.

Now we have to go thru the *haj mabrur* – 'blessed haj' games – everybody visiting everybody else and they give you these little thimbles of water from Zamzam, which is supposed to have some sort of healing and purifying effects on the soul or whatever. People, I want to be the person who does the documentary showing that the Saudi government has been extending the life of that well by adding *tap water* to it. Some Hajis who see me smile when they are giving these little bottles of blessed water as presents decide that a praying rug would be better. They will have to start me on the road to redemption in the first place and they think a flying carpet from Mecca will be my fast track to Jennah ('heaven').

My blasphemous ranting aside, becoming a Haj is a big deal. It is an exhausting couple of weeks and anybody who commits him/herself to such an ordeal has at least earned the right to get a special name – and Haji has a nice ring to it. Personally, I've decided to go to Mecca as late in my life as possible. You see, if the *tabula rasa* part of the Haj is right and there is a 'God', it makes sense to live life like a pig, *then* go purify your soul in Mecca and live your last days like a saint. I have it all worked out. That is my contingency plan for the remote possibility of the existence of a deity.

A reader sent me an angry e-mail a couple of days ago (not 'a reader' who writes in the comments, someone else) asking me why I dislike the 'human shields' so much. He/she actually asked 'Why do you spit on them?' Ewww. Now, I was never *that* unfriendly. I have not met any of them in person (which just might happen in the next couple of days), but what I dislike is the idea. But since dissing them gets people so excited, here we go and do what Destiny's Child don't, 'cause their mamma taught them better than that: we be dissing the shields *again* on the Internet.

One of the latest groups to arrive in Baghdad, mostly Europeans, was welcomed to the al-Rasheed Hotel, which is like the Waldorf Astoria of Baghdad – no other hotel is more expensive and exclusive. All of them were wearing T-shirts with what was supposed to be *Human Shields* in Arabic, but they had it all wrong. It said *Adra'a Basharia*, instead of *Duru'u Basharia*, which got them a few giggles and a new name: they are now known as the *Adra'a*, just to show how clueless they are. A lot of funny Arabic these days with all these Human Shields running around. A van with a foreign number plate standing near the Ministry of Information has *No War* written all over it in many languages, the biggest in Arabic. All over the front it says *La Harba*, which is wrong and sounds like a nightclub. My cousin thought it was cute.

Anyway, what really got my goat this time was finding out that the Human Shields get food coupons worth 15,000 dinars per meal – three for every day. Fifteen thousand!

Do you know how much the monthly food ration for a four-person family is worth – for a whole month, not *per meal* (at real cost, not subsidized)?

30,000 dinars – if you get someone to buy the bad rice they give you for a decent price.

And the Human Shields get 15,000! What are they eating? A whole lamb every meal? Let's put this within context. Today in the morning, Raed, our friend G. and I went for a late big breakfast. We had two *tishreeb bagilas* (can't explain that – you have to be an Iraqi to get it, otherwise it sounds inedible) and a *makhlama* (an omelette with minced meat), tea, fizzy drinks and *argila* afterwards (the water-pipe-thingy) all for 4,750 dinars – and we were not going super-cheap. A lunch in any above-average restaurant will not be more than 8,000 dinars and that includes *everything*. 15,000 is a meal in a super-expensive restaurant in Arasat Street, in one of those places that really almost have an ONLY FOREIGNERS ALLOWED, NO IRAQIS WELCOME UNLESS YOU ARE UN STAFF sign on it. I will stop calling them 'tourist' when they stop taking all this pampering from the Iraqi government. Did I tell you about the tours? Today it was Babylon. You are really missing it. It's the cheapest way to do the Iraq trip you have always wanted to do, but were too scared.

And I have a tip for all freelance journalists who are not getting their visas: join the Human Shields. It's the best way to get past the visa thing. Every third one of these 'shields' will be writing an article somewhere. Hurry! Contact your local 'war tourism' travel agent!

Sorry, I just don't get it. What *are* they doing here?

So, that should get me enough hate mail for the next couple of days.

Enough of that. TV time. The biggest TV event last week was the first *Waznak Thahab* (*Your Weight in Gold*) show with Noor al-Sharif (no relation to Omar) as host. Noor is a very serious Egyptian actor – I linked to one of his shows in a post I wrote last Ramadan. This is his first as show host and he totally blew it – he looked scared and nervous. The contestants were calmer and cooler than him, we used to have Aiman Zedan, who is a Syrian actor, do the show and he was a killer. The show is actually on Abu Dhabi TV, but our Youth TV just steals it off the air and shows it the next day. State-sanctioned piracy – what else can you wish for?

:: salam 7:17 PM [+] ::

Tuesday, 25 February 2003

You know what my favourite part in the last two resolutions on Iraq is? The part where it says 'DECIDES to remain seized of the matter'.+ Oooh, can't wait for the next episode of *UN Drama*, the best show this side of the Milky Way.

+ www.nytimes.com.

You would have thought that an almost-war-declaration would have more dramatic wording than:

> **ACTING under Chapter VII of the Charter of the United Nations, DECIDES that Iraq has failed to take the final opportunity afforded it in Resolution 1441 (2002).**

They definitely need a better script writer for that show, but I guess that is what CNN and the rest are for.

The wise oracle of Gotham✝ predicts that You-Know-Who will be history by the 18th of March, but she won't say how she got that date. C'mon, spill it! Whatwhywhere? And she also invited me to tea at the Palm Court if I ever came to NYC. Alrighty, who said you can't get a classy date thru the Internet?

:: **salam 10:58 AM [+]** ::

✝ Diana, at www.letterfromgotham.blogspot.com.

Saturday, 1 March 2003

It is nice to see the Office of the Iraq Oil-for-Food program rise to the occasion and redo their site. With all the attention it is going to get if the program stays intact after an 'invasion', they really needed a better image. Their site looked hideous. Now they have this nifty map and even pictures. Go take a look.**+**

:: **salam 11:41 AM [+]** ::

Sunday, 2 March 2003

I wasn't going to write about this, but since the *Guardian* has mentioned it, I won't be giving away any state secrets.

Have you read this article on the *Guardian*'s website: 'The big match unites a country of two halves: Luke Harding, in Irbil, sees a top Baghdad soccer team take on Kurdish.'

It's just a filler, nothing really interesting, and if you did read it you probably just skimmed over this paragraph:

> **To reach Irbil, the Baghdad players had to travel across a reinforced Iraqi frontline, past freshly dug army trenches filled with oil, and up into the mountains of Kurdistan.**

Blink and you miss it. You still didn't see it? Listen: Freshly. Dug. Army. Trenches. *Filled with oil.*

+ un.org/depts/oip.

Story time: A week ago on the way to work I saw a huge column of blackest-black smoke coming from the direction of the Dorah refinery, which is within Baghdad city limits – thought nothing of it really. A couple of weeks earlier to that, a fuel tank near the Rasheed army camp exploded and it looked the same – stuff like that happens. My father was driving thru the area later and he said it looked like they were burning excess or wasted oil. Well, they were never environmentalists to start with – if they didn't burn it, they would have dumped it in the river or something.

The smoke was there for three days and the column could be seen from all over Baghdad being dragged in a line across the sky by the winds. During the same time and on the same road I take to work, I see two HUGE trenches being dug. It looked like they were going to put some sort of machinery in it, wide enough for a truck to drive thru and would easily take three big trucks.

A couple of days after the smoke-show over Baghdad, I and my father are going past these trenches and we see oil being dumped into the trenches. You could hear my brain going into action. My father gave me the shut-up-u-nutty-paranoid-freak look, but I knew it was true. The last two days everybody talks about it. They are planning to make a smoke-screen of some sorts using black crude oil. Actually, rumour has it that they have been experimenting with various fuel mixtures to see what would produce the blackest, vilest smoke and the three days of smoke from Dorah was the final test.

Around Baghdad they would probably go roughly along the green belt, which was conceived to stop the sandstorms coming from the western deserts. I have no idea how a smoke-screen can be of any use, except make sure that the people in Baghdad die of asphyxiation and covered in soot. I think I will be getting those gas masks after all.

FunFact: After the oil wells in Kuwait were set on fire and the whole region covered in the blackest and ugliest cloud, it rained for days on Baghdad, washing everything with black water from the sky – the marks took a year to wash out. I think Salman Rushdie would have found this very amusing. Characters in his novels are always haunted by things past in the strangest ways, the shame of your actions following you and then washing you with its black water –

no ablutions for you, Mr H., watch your city covered with the shame of your actions. We have an expression – *skham wijih* – which roughly translates to 'face covered with soot' and is used to describe someone who has done something utterly disgraceful. Getting your city covered with *skham* once has to haunt you for the rest of your life; but now we get *Skham from the Sky II: The Return of the Evil Cloud*. The world is just a re-run of bad movies, but Mr W. Bush already beat me to that expression.

:: salam 12:35 PM [+] ::

Wednesday, 5 March 2003

Bigger, better, faster – so stop harassing me about the font size. And I promise I will have a proper post later today. I have been a bit lazy. My mind is full of fuzz and number 18s – that's your fault. It *is* a super cool idea really, and will fit with so many conspiracy theories type of stuff, but you'll have to make her tell you about it on the 19th.[+]

Since last night Google.com and msn.com are blocked. All the usual news sites are still accessible – even Google news, only the search gets you the YOUR ACCESS HAS BEEN DENIED page.

:: salam 11:03 AM [+] ::

Thursday, 6 March 2003

Article in the CSmonitor.com.[++] You see that woman on the right of the pic? Her name is not Janon, as the article says, it is Jinan (it means 'heavens') and she is the evil witch of the Department of Architecture. You can see it in her smile. The woman on the left makes the whole engineering college march to her whistle. Really very strong and well-known women in the College of Engineering. One of them has a very eloquent daughter apparently:

'I hope they see us as people,' says the increasingly anxious Nihal,

----
+ This refers to Gotham's oracle: www.letterfromgotham.blogspot.com.
++ 'US-taught Iraqis feel war's weight' (5 March 2003) by Scott Peterson (www.csmonitor.com/2003/0305/p01s04-woiq.html).

in a separate interview. 'It's a feeling you can't describe. You worry about yourself and your family and aunts and uncles in their houses – it's like your heart is in a million pieces all over the place and you don't know how to keep it together.'

And Jinan kicks ass too:

'It's funny,' she says of the cultural disconnect. 'Why should we be sitting here trying to convince you that we are OK? Why should I have to make you feel like we are people worth living?'

The dinar is miraculously keeping its cool and is still around the 2,360 for a dollar. The lowest it ever got during the last ten years was 2,500 for a dollar, but I think we will hit that bottom in the next couple of weeks. A relative of mine who works at a bank says that everybody who comes into the bank is complaining that *al suq waguf* ('the market is at a standstill'). They are a 'private bank' – there is no such thing as a private bank really, they are all partially owned by the state – and have been told to stock up on biscuits, dates and water. Can't imagine why – as if anyone is going to come to work when things start dropping on our heads. But to be fair, after Gulf War I the banks opened pretty fast. People who lived near their workplace and could walk to work did just that. The banks limited the amount you are allowed to take from your account to 100 dinars, which was around $200 or so at the time. Today, 100 dinars buys me a pack of local chemical-flavour bubble gum.

Since we are talking about money, today was pay-day. It is amazing what the sentence 'We're sorry, but you know how things are at the moment blah blah blah' can do to your paycheck. In one single year I have gone down from $200 to $100 and hit rock bottom at $50. In retrospect, deciding to go back to living with my parents was the wisest decision I have made for quite a while. My friend G. is getting half his salary in money and the rest in alcohol – really, no joke. But good imported stuff which we wouldn't buy anyway. His fatcat-filthy-rich boss turned seriously Muslim and is giving away his stash of the devil's beverages. Good for us, I say.

Human Shields Bashing #124

'Basically, they said we are not going to feed you any longer,' said

John Ross, an American who has been active in radical causes since he tore up his draft card in 1964.⁺

Excuse while I wipe the tears from my eyes. Out! Out! Out! He could have at least said something more in line with his 'radical cause'. This is a bit insulting, actually. For some reason I feel offended. FEED YOU? Why does the Iraqi government have to friggin' feed you? You have volunteered to 'help' in a country which can't feed its own population properly (well, it could if it spent a bit less on people like *you*).

There is another good bit:

The activists accused the Iraqi authorities of trying to use them as pawns in the war with America.

Oh, shockhorror! What a surprise! Back to where you came from. Don't wait for thank-you speeches – Out! Out! Out!

The bitter flight from Iraq follows a showdown with the Iraqi authorities *who demanded that they decamp from their hotels in central Baghdad and take up their self-assigned roles as civilian protectors.*

No no, just stay in your hotels, buy souvenirs and make fun of the backward ways of these Iraqis. Hope you sent all your friends postcards telling them about the pitta and tahini you have been eating while strolling around Baghdad, you tourists. Did you take enough pictures of children begging in the streets to show your friends back home how much you care about the plight of the poor in the Third World? Bet they were all shaking hands and promising to see each other at the next 'worthy cause' party.

Today is *mumarasa* ('practice') day in Baghdad. (~~Maybe tomorrow too~~ nope, I checked, it was a one-day thing.) All the security forces – police, civil defence units and the like, excluding the army – are going thru the motions. Besides parading up and down all over the country, all units were supposed to go thru the events of an 'emergency situation'. The funniest were the policemen. They have been issued army helmets with green camouflage fluff on it. All the main

----

⁺ 'Human Shield cracks on Baghdad's cynicism' (3 March 2003) by Suzanne Goldenberg (www.guardian.co.uk).

squares and intersections had at least twelve people wearing their full gear, carrying Kalashnikovs and a couple of extra ammunition magazines. There were also fire-fighting guys with big red cars *and* Kalashnikovs – everybody gets to carry guns (I don't get where the myth that fire-fighters are sexy came from). And other assorted killing machines mounted on cars: some were going around the city, some were stationed. They all looked a bit self-conscious and hot because of the helmets. It was around 24°C at noon today – pretty warm to be wearing all the stuff they had on.

People in Basra are saying that for them it does feel like war already – lots of raids down there. A couple of days ago in the seven o'clock local news bulletin they showed a number of Baath Party members overseeing the burning of leaflets (the ones that look like $100 bills). They only said it was in the southern parts of Iraq. I wish someone can bring me one of them. Imagine the eBay potential it would have in a couple of months' time.

There is an incredibly strong rumour that Uday is in Russia (Belorussia). What makes it even more suspicious is this: I wrote that Google was blocked from last night, well now it is open, but type a search for anything in Russia and you get the ACCESS DENIED page on the search results.

And have you seen the speech by Izat Ibrahim[+] in the Islamic Summit today? Was that diplomacy in action or what? Calling the Kuwaiti foreign minister a monkey – he actually called him a monkey – and insulting his 'moustache' – a very serious offence in Bedouin code, like insulting his manly pride – we have a master in abuse-hurling in our government. Although Libya and Saudi Arabia did quite well a couple of days earlier. And they ask why the Arab nations are such a farce. It is because we have kings and presidents who behave like kids in a sandpit.

:: **salam 1:22 AM [+]** ::

[+] The Iraqi Vice-President.

Sunday, 9 March 2003

Tips on how to become super popular in the office:

Listen to what everybody is talking about, then surprise them with cool info from the web. It helps if Google is still blocked and no one has yet figured out that there is life after Google. Today, the million-dollar question was 'Who the hell is Barbara Bodine?'[+] Well the ones who listen to the BBC World Service were asking, the rest were just going what-what-what?

> **The plan calls for a northern and southern sector to be administered by two retired US Army generals, sources said. A central sector, including Baghdad, will be administered by *Barbara Bodine*, a former US ambassador to Yemen, the sources said.[++]**

We will for the moment try to ignore whether this means a divided Iraq or federalism thrust down our throats or a redraw of the Iraqi map, because this will be, after all, the decision of the ~~invaders~~ liberators. We have the right to remain silent otherwise we get smacked upside the head.

Anyway, www.dogpile.com came to the rescue and I was the Internet superhero when I showed them THIS[+++] – and more oohs and aaahs when I showed them THIS.[*] I should have charged 250 dinars for each viewing. Actually the biggest surprise was finding out that Barbara Bodine was in Iraq in 1983 as Deputy Principal Officer in the US embassy here.

General reactions? You can imagine the fear of castration the Iraqi males are going thru at the moment. Don't expect this to be swallowed very easily. And to divert this unease they would just say something along the lines 'She doesn't look very pretty, does she?' One person who doesn't actually work here, but was dragged by a colleague to see the picture, said 'You know, it is their intention to

----

[+] Barbara Bodine, the former US ambassador to Yemen who served in Baghdad in the 1980s, was appointed to look after the central region, including Baghdad, after Gulf War II. She was held hostage at the US embassy in Kuwait during Gulf War I.

[++] 'Three US administrators will run post-war Iraq' by Barbara Starr, 7 March 2003 (www.cnn.com).

[+++] Biography of Barbara Bodine on www.state.gov.

[*] Photograph of Barbara Bodine on cnni.co.uk.

destroy the pride of the Muslim man.' Tread carefully, is what I say. Change shouldn't be plunked on people's heads like this, especially when there is already an atmosphere of mistrust and unfriendliness. Someone said this will be like having another Gertrude Bell,[+] I am not sure this is good. (Two interesting links: The Female Lawrence of Arabia and The Gertrude Bell Project[++] with an amazing photo library. Thanks a million for the link A. – he is the only Iraqi reader I have, apparently.)

:: **salam 11:49 AM [+]** ::

A BBC reporter walking thru the Mutanabi Friday book market (again) ends his report with: 'It looks like Iraqis are putting on an air of normality.'

Look, what are you supposed to do? Run around in the streets wailing? War is at the door eeeeeeeeeeeee! Besides, this 'normality' doesn't go very deep. Almost everything is more expensive than it was a couple of months ago; people are digging wells in their gardens; on the radio yesterday, after playing a million songs from the time of the war with Iran (these are like cartoon theme songs for people my age, we know them all by heart), they read out instructions on how to make a trench and prepare for war – that is after President Saddam advised Iraqis to make these trenches in their gardens.

But in order not to disappoint the BBC, me, Raed and G. put on our 'normal' faces and went to buy CDs from Arasat Street in a demonstration of normality. After going first into Sandra's fruit juice shop and getting what people from Foreign would probably call a poor imitation of a banana and apple smoothie, we spent half an hour contemplating the CD racks at music shop. Raed, being the master of talk-and-slurp-at-the-same-time technique, was trying to steal away my 'normality' by reminding me that I will be wasting my

----

[+] The archaeologist Gertrude Bell (1868–1926) learned Arabic and travelled deep into the desert to investigate ancient archaeological sites. Her knowledge of the country and its tribes made her a prime target for recruitment by British Intelligence during the First World War. Later, as a political officer and then as Oriental Secretary to the High Commissioner in Baghdad, she became a king-maker in the new state of Iraq, which she helped to create. As Honorary Director of Antiquities in Iraq, she established the Iraq Museum in Baghdad.

[++] www.gerty.ncl.ac.uk/home.

10,000 dinars because there will be no electricity for the CD player. I explained to him that I am planning on operating a pirate radio station and need to stock on music for the masses I plan to entertain – said in a matter of fact voice and Raed didn't even blink, which made Mr Music Shop Owner look at us very suspiciously at this point, so we moved to the next rack. But since I buy the stuff that would otherwise sit and collect dust, he didn't say much and was very happy to take away 12,500 dinars. I bought five instead of the planned four CDs – many thanks to Malaysian bootleggers for providing us with cheap CDs. The Deftones, Black Rebel Motorcycle Club, Erykah Badu and the new Amr Diab (here+ for audio clips if you are interested) have joined the Pax Radio CD racks.

Other normal stuff we did this week:
- Finished taping all the windows in the house – actually a very relaxing exercise, if you forget why you are doing it in the first place.
- Installed a manual pump on the well we have dug, because up till now we had an electrical pump on it.
- Bought 60 litres of gasoline to run the small electricity generator we have. Bought two nifty kerosene cookers and stocked loads of kerosene and dug holes in the garden to bury the stuff so that the house doesn't turn into a bomb.
- Prepared one room for emergency nasty attacks and bought 'particle masks' – that's what it says on the box – for use if they light those oil trenches. The masks just might stop our lungs from becoming tar pits. They are very hot items since the word on the trenches spread. You can buy one for 250 dinars and they are selling faster than the hot cakes of Bab-al-agha.
- Got two rooms in our house ready to welcome our first IDPs (internally displaced persons): my youngest aunt, a single mom with three kids, because she lives farthest away from the rest of us and another aunt from Karbala in the south. Hotel Pax is officially open for the season. No need to make reservations, but you might need to bring a mattress if you come too late.

+ www.erykahbadu.com and www.amrdiab.net.

Other news/rumours:

Party members are going around the city telling people to stay in their homes if anything happens. 'Do not go out in the street.' 'Everything will be brought to you.' They have dug wells in many places with generators beside them to pump the water out and they will be distributing the water. If there is a need to move out of the house, wait until the Party car comes to take you.

They have gone around and asked which households own more than one car, taken down names and numbers – rumour has it that they are going to appropriate any extra car if the need arises. Anyway, you will not be able to drive your car around. People like doctors in state hospitals have been given badges to stick on their cars and so have Party members. You will have to have some sort of permission to move around when the curfew takes place the moment an attack starts. Because of that, we have issued our own curfew from last Friday. Headcount at 10.30 p.m. With so many people in the house a roll-call is the only way to make sure everybody is here. And we are counting on the Americans to attack at night. If they start the attack during the day, they would have mayhem on the streets.

:: **salam 6:43 PM [+]** ::

Tuesday, 11 March 2003

Some time ago I promised to show you the new 10,000 dinar bill. It has been issued around four months ago and might become a part of this country's history soon.

Please excuse the quality. I don't have the scanner at home. What you see beside the picture of the Prez is the Unknown Soldier monument in Baghdad.

The dinar hit a new low tonight: $1=2,700 dinars. The wholesale markets in Shorjah stopped buying and selling today, to see which way the dinar will move next.

:: salam 2:41 AM [+] ::

In one of my posts I wrote that I seem to have only one Iraqi reader. Well, I was wrong. I have two and a half (half-Iraqi, half-Chinese). What is really exciting is that the second reader is a girl here in Baghdad. She's twenty-three years old and is a computer geek (well, engineer) and she agreed to write something for the blog. She will go by the name 'riverbend'. Please give her a warm welcome. I hope she decides to join the weblog and write as often as she can in the next couple of weeks.

So, without further ado, I give you 'riverbend':

Salam, you've reminded me that we have to get to duct-taping the windows (did you use an 'X' pattern or the traditional '*'?). [*Salam: The * star is good, but with particularly big windows I have been using a + and Xs in each quadrant.*] We've all been talking about the war, discussing the possibilities, implications, etc. but it really hit me yesterday when I got home and – 'lo and behold!' – there were no pictures or paintings on the walls! So I asked, stupidly, 'Where are all the pictures?' I was told that they've been 'put away', because who knew what might come tumbling down if a bomb fell particularly close? I then pointed to a funky black steel chandelier that no one seems to pay any attention to and reminded them that it should be a more immediate worry, not the pictures . . . It is beginning to look like a Gothic death trap. I have visions of it coming down on my head . . .

Otherwise, yes, we are living normally – going to work, cleaning house, eating, drinking. Life doesn't stand still every time America threatens war. It gets more difficult, true enough, but it goes on – which, by the way, is driving the foreign journalists crazy. They want some action here and seeing people go about their daily lives is just a waste of time and film, it seems.

Be careful with the gasoline, Salam. A whole family burned to death the other day because their gasoline storing facilities weren't adequate (is that considered 'friendly fire'?) – hope you've got it stored in a safe place. [*Salam: Yeah, we saw that on TV. Pretty nasty – my mother freaked, of course.*] We've stocked up on candles (dozens of 'em), but my mother is starting to eye my collection of scented candles anyway. So you can anticipate the scene – hundreds of bombs flying overhead, the deafening sound of planes, blended with murmured prayers, in a semi-dark room smelling faintly of . . . lavender. And that smell will forever be consecrated in my mind, along with the rest of the 'war memories': candles, duct tape, kerosene lamps and lavender . . .

On a not-quite-completely-different subject: I had a flash of déjà vu this morning while reading the news. *sigh* Aren't the Americans *ever* going to get tired of war?

riverbend

The next time, if 'riverbend' decides to join, she will be part of this group blog (yes, it was supposed to be a group blog, but Raed is such a lazy bastard). I'll be happy to forward any mail to her until she makes up her mind whether to put her addy here or not.

:: **salam 1:30 PM [+]** ::

Wednesday, 12 March 2003

Here is something fun to read – unlike the comments down below where we engage in index-finger wagging at each other. This I got from Douglas, who has always been thoughtful and sends me articles from French magazines or newspapers translated. Thanks Douglas. This one is exceptionally good. It is about events before the first Gulf War.

If *vous parlez français*, then go to this link: *Un après-midi avec Saddam.*✦

If you are no-French-please, then go to this link. I hope I have not

----
✦ An article by Alcibiades Hidalgo in the French newspaper *Le Monde*, 11 March 2003 (www.lemonde.fr).

done a *faux pas* by posting your translation, Douglas: 'An Afternoon with Saddam'.⁺ It is on an abandoned blog.

My favourite bits:

> . . . blah blah blah . . . **'You can tell comrade Fidel Castro,' he (Saddam Hussein) said, getting up, 'that I thank him for his solicitude. If the troops of the United States invade Iraq, we shall crush them like that!' he concluded resoundingly, stamping the carpet several times with his shining military boots . . . The audience had ended . . . blah blah blah . . . Without asking us to repeat what happened again, he (Fidel Castro) only asked the Gallego to imitate with his own feet the gesture with which Saddam had shown how he would crush the Americans.**

It's like watching two kids talking about a fight in the playground: me crush you like a cock-a-roach, youyou!

We'd rather not talk about who crushed who. As for the next 'Mother of All Battles' . . . one word: shock'n'awe. Learn it in Arabic: *al-ithara wa al-faza*. That's like putting stones in the middle of mud-cakes and throwing them at me, cheater.

:: **salam 12:49 PM [+]** ::

Thursday, 13 March 2003

Today is a public holiday. In the Muslim calendar it is the 10th of Muharam – or Ashura (3ashura2) for Shia Muslims. A pivotal date in the history of Shia. Today is the day Imam Hussein was killed in Karbala/Iraq. Which, in the words of Shiapundit⁺⁺ 'is a time for grief, reflection, and *ibadat* (prayers). Nothing else.'

My mother is Shia from Karbala, so each year we wake up in the morning (it is 1 a.m. as I write this) to the sound of the 3azah al 7ussain ('The Lament of Hussein') from the radio – not very pleasant. And after that we hear the stories of the public laments that used to take place in Karbala (now they are banned). The last three days of the Imam's life are acted out throughout the whole city of

----
⁺ A link to The Pointless Linkage Project:
pointlesslinkage.blogspot.com/2003_03_09_pointlesslinkage_archive.html#90576946.
⁺⁺ www.shiapundit.blogspot.com.

Karbala. I'll give you an idea of these last few days. I hope the Shia readers will excuse me if I don't get it fully right:

Basically, it is the story of the battle between Imam Hussein, the grandson of the prophet Mohammed, and Caliph Yazid on the Kerbala desert in 680 AD.

Imam Hussein is to return to Kufa/Iraq after he has been reassured that the people there will help him in his struggle – after he had fled to Mecca under the threat of being assassinated by Yazid's people. On his way back, the horse he is riding stops at a certain place near the Euphrates and doesn't move. When the Imam asks the name of this place he is told it is the desert of Karbala (karrun wa bala2), which roughly means 'harm and calamity'. He tells his followers that this is the place where he will be killed, as prophesied. Tents are put up and they are very soon after that surrounded by Yazid's army. The Imam does not have many people with him and most of them are family members with women and children. We'll move a bit quickly thru the events now.

First their water supply is cut off for three days and then the battle starts. Family members of the Imam die one after the other trying to protect Imam Hussein, including his young sons. After all the men have been killed, Yazid's army moves thru the camp and burns down the tents. Imam Hussein's head is then taken to Damascus to prove to Yazid that al-Hussein has been killed.

Now, imagine this being enacted in real life thru the whole city, to this day. There is a district in Karbala called Mukhayam ('the camp'), which actually used to be the site of the tents for the play. The most hated role that had to be played is the role of the soldier who will kill Imam al-Hussein. My aunt tells me it usually ends with the people running after him throwing stones, until he hides in one of the houses. Groups of lamenters would then move thru the city, from the scary – groups of people hitting themselves with whips on their backs for not being there to help al-Hussein in his tragedy – to the poetry-reading groups of students, to the solemn lawyers. People would come from all over Iraq and from as far as Pakistan to join with their own lamenters. In houses and mosques you would see loads of men and women listening to the *maqtal* ('the killing of Hussein'), beating their chests and crying. There is even special food for these days cooked in the streets.

I have seen nothing of this ever. It has been banned for as long as I can remember. It is considered a public unauthorized demonstration. Laments can be held in houses, but not the big play in the streets of Karbala. Lately, even the cooking of *qima* (minced meat with chickpeas) and *Harissa* (something which looks a bit like gruel, actually) in public has been banned. My aunt, who just came from Karbala today, said that the army is all around Karbala, which happens every year.

:: salam 2:17 AM [+] ::

Saturday, 15 March 2003

The big momma of all demonstrations is going on and I will be stuck in the office for ever. Maybe I will take a walk and watch the show. Operation 'Office Evac' is now in its final phase. Any day now.

:: salam 10:30 AM [+] ::

Sunday, 16 March 2003

RANT

No one inside Iraq is for war (note I said 'war', not 'a change of regime'). No human being in his right mind will ask you to give him the beating of his life – unless you are a member of Fight Club, that is – and if you *do* hear Iraqis (in Iraq, not expat) saying 'Come on, bomb us!' it is the exasperation and ten years of sanctions and hardship talking. There is no person **inside** Iraq who will be jumping up and down asking for the bombs to drop. We are not suicidal, you know – not all of us in any case.

I think that the coming war is not justified (and it is very near now, we hear the war drums loud and clear – if you don't, then take those earplugs off!). The excuses for it have been stretched to their limits they will almost snap. A decision has been made sometime ago that 'regime change' in Baghdad is needed and excuses for the forceful change have to be made. I do think war could have been avoided. Not by running back and forth the last two months, that's silly. But the whole issue of Iraq should have been dealt with differently since the first day after Gulf War I.

The entities that call themselves 'the international community' should have assumed their responsibilities a long time ago; should have thought about what the sanctions they have imposed really meant; should have looked at reports about weapons and human rights abuses a long time before having them thrown in their faces as excuses for war five minutes before midnight.

What is bringing on this rant is the question that has been bugging me for days now: how could 'support democracy in Iraq' come to mean 'bomb the hell out of Iraq'? Why did it end up that democracy won't happen unless we go thru war? Nobody minded an un-democratic Iraq for a very long time. Now people have decided to bomb us to democracy? Well, thank you! How thoughtful.

The situation in Iraq could have been solved in other ways than what the world will be going thru the next couple of weeks. It can't have been that impossible. Look at the northern parts of Iraq – that is a model that has worked quite well. Why wasn't anybody interested in doing that in the south? Just like the ~~US/UK~~ UN created a protected area there, why couldn't the model be tried in the south? It would have cut off the regime's arms and legs. And once the people see what they have been deprived of they will not be willing to go back. Just ask any Iraqi from the Kurdish areas.

Instead the world watched while after the war the Shias were crushed by Saddam's army in a manner that really didn't happen before the Gulf War. Does anyone else see the words 'Iran/not in the US interest' floating or is it me hallucinating?

And there is the matter of sanctions. Now that Iraq has been thru a decade of these sanctions, I can only hope that their effects are clear enough for them not to be tried upon another nation. Sanctions, which allegedly should have kept a potentially dangerous situation in Iraq in check, brought a whole nation to its knees instead. And who ultimately benefited from the sanctions? Neither the international community nor the Iraqi people, but *he* who was in power and control still is. These sanctions made the Iraqi people hostages in the hands of this regime; tightened an already tight noose around our necks. A whole nation, a proud and learned nation, was devastated not by the war, but by sanctions. Our brightest and most creative minds fled the country not because of oppression alone, but because no one inside Iraq could make a living or survive. And can anyone tell me what the sanctions really did about weapons? Get real. There are always willing nations who will help; there are always organizations which will find his money sweet. Oil-for-Food? Smart Sanctions? Get a clue. Who do you think is getting all those contracts to supply the people with 'food'? Who do you think is heaping money in bank accounts abroad? It is *his* people, *his* family and the people who play *his* game – abroad and in Iraq; Iraqis and non-Iraqis.

What I mean to say is that things could have been different. I can't help look at the northern parts of Iraq with envy and wonder why.

Do support democracy in Iraq, but don't equate it with war. What will happen is something that could/should have been avoided. Don't expect me to wear a 'I ♥ Bush' T-shirt. Support democracy in Iraq, not by bombing us to hell and then trying to build it up again (well, that is going to happen anyway), not by sending human shields (let's be real, the war is going to happen and Saddam will use you as hostages), but by keeping an eye on what will happen after the war.

Support Democracy in Iraq

To end this rant, a word about Islamic fundis/wahabisim/qaeda and all that.

Do you know when the sight of women veiled from top to bottom became common in cities in Iraq? Do you know when the question of segregation between boys and girls became red hot? When tribal law replaced THE LAW? When 'Wahabi'✦ became part of our vocabulary?

✦ A Wahabi is a member of a sect of Muslim puritans following strictly the original words of the Koran. They are named after Muhammad ibn Abd-el-Wahhab, who founded the sect in the eighteenth century.

It only happened *after* the Gulf War. I think it was Cheney or Albright who said they will bomb Iraq back to the Stone Age . . . Well, you did. Iraqis have never accepted religious extremism in their lives. They still don't. Wahabis in their short *dishdasha* are still looked upon as sheep who have strayed from the herd. But they are spreading. The combination of poverty/no work/low self-esteem and the bitterness of seeing people who rose to riches and power without any real merit (but having the right family name or connection) shook the whole social fabric. Situations which would have been unacceptable in the past are being tolerated today.

They call it *al hamla al imania* ('the religious campaign'). Of course, it was supported by the Government: pumping them with words like 'poor in this life, rich in heaven' kept the people quiet. Or the other side of the coin is getting paid by Wahabi organizations. Come pray and get paid – no joke, dead serious. If the Government can't give you a job, run to the nearest mosque and they will pay and support you. This never happened before. It's outrageous. But what are people supposed to do? Their government is denied funds to pay proper wages and what they get is funnelled into their pockets. So please stop telling me about the fundis – never knew what they are never would have seen them in my streets.

RANT ENDS

:: salam 1:37 AM [+] ::

Monday, 17 March 2003

Impossibly long lines in front of gas stations last night – some even had two police cars in front of them to make sure no 'incidents' occur.

The price of bottled water jumped up threefold.

On Shabab TV (Youth TV) there were announcements that the NUIS[+] is selling water pumps and tanks, hard helmets, small electrical generators and, most surreally, chemical-biological attack protection chambers – in the picture they showed it looked like an octagonal barrel laid on its side, with two bunks in it and

----
+ National Union of Iraqi Students.

some strange equipment on the outside. No prices, just a phone number.

Rumours of defaced pictures of Saddam in Dorah and Thawra districts (maybe, maybe not). And the cities of Rawa and Anna are so full of people now you wouldn't find a hut to rent. It was pretty safe to be there during Gulf War I and people who have the money are renting places there, hoping that it will be safe this time.

The dinar is hovering around the 2,700 per dollar and the hottest items after the 'particle-masks', are earplugs – they can't be found in shops and you have to pre-order.

:: salam 8:48 AM [+] ::

Wednesday, 19 March 2003

I would have posted something earlier today, but there was a lot to do and my brother reminded me that we have to go refill the car, and that was two hours of wasted time waiting. It is not as bad as two days ago, but the gas stations are still crowded. A couple of hours after I wrote that two police cars were standing near gas stations to keep things in order, we went out again and there were more Party members wearing their olive-green uniforms with Kalashnikovs in gas stations, but today it is back to the police cars. There is a rumour that they will open the 'special' gas stations for the public too. There are four of these in Baghdad, used only by *them* or whoever has the right ID.

Before I go into what was going on today, I really want to thank all the people who have been sending e-mails and letting me know that they care and worry about what will happen in Iraq. Thank you so much. I hope you understand that it takes a bit of time to answer your questions, so please don't be angry if I don't reply promptly. I print them out for Raed to read and he is totally baffled. Some of them I wish I could publish or print and paste on lamp-posts. Thank you very much.

A couple of weeks ago, journalists were exasperated by that fact that Iraqis just went on with their lives and did not panic. Well, today there is a very different picture. It is actually a bit scary and very disturbing. To start with, the dinar hit another low: 3,100 dinars per dollar. There was no exchange place open. If you went and asked, they just looked at you as if you were crazy. Wherever you go you see closed shops and it is not just doors-locked closed, but sheet-metal-welded-on-the-front closed; windows-removed-and-built-with-bricks closed; doors were being welded shut. There were trucks loaded with all sorts of stuff being taken from the shops to wherever their owner had a secure place. Houses which are still being built are having huge walls erected in front of them with no doors, to make sure they don't get used as barracks I guess. Driving thru Mansour, Harthiya or Arasat is pretty depressing. Still, me, Raed and G. went out to have our last lunch together.

The radio plays war songs from the 1980s non-stop. We know them all by heart. Driving thru Baghdad now, singing along to songs saying things like 'we will be with you till the day we die, Saddam' was suddenly a bit too heavy. No one gave that line too much thought, but somehow these days it sounds sinister, since last night one of the most played old 'patriotic' songs was the song of the youth *al-fituuwa*: it is the code that all Fedayeen✢ should join their assigned units. And it is still being played.

A couple of hours earlier we were at a shop and a woman said as she was leaving (and this is a very common sentence): *itha allah khalana taibeen* ('We'll see you tomorrow, if God keeps us alive') – and the whole place just freezes. She laughed nervously and said she didn't mean *that*, and we all laughed, but these things start having a meaning beyond being figures of speech.

There still is no military presence in the streets, but we expect that to happen after the ultimatum. Here and there you see cars with machine-guns going around the streets, but not too many. Enough to make you nervous.

The prices of things are going higher and higher, not only because of the drop of the dinar, but because there is no more supply. Businesses are shutting down and packing up. Only the small stores are open.

Pharmacies are very helpful in getting you the supplies you need, but they also have only a limited amount of medication and first-aid

----
✢ Fighters loyal to Saddam Hussein.

stuff. So if you have not bought what you need you might have to pay inflated prices.

And if you want to run off to Syria, the trip will cost you $600. It used to be $50. It's cheaper to stay now. Anyway, we went past the travel-permit issuing offices and they were shut with lock and chain.

Some rumours:

It is being said that Barazan (Saddam's brother) has suggested to him that he should do the decent thing and surrender. He got himself under house arrest in one of the presidential palaces which is probably going to be one of the first to be hit.

Families of bigwigs and *his* own family are being armed to the teeth. More from fear of Iraqis seeking retribution than Americans.

And by the smell of it we are going to have a sandstorm today, which means that the people on the borders are already covered in sand. Crazy weather. Yesterday it rains and today sand.

:: **salam 3:13 AM [+]** ::

Thursday, 20 March 2003

It is even too late for last-minute things to buy – there are too few shops open. We went again for a drive thru Baghdad's main streets. Too depressing. I have never seen Baghdad like this. Today the Baath Party people started taking their places in the trenches and main squares and intersections, fully armed and freshly shaven. They looked too clean and well groomed to defend anything. And the most shocking thing was the number of kids. They couldn't be older than twenty, sitting in trenches sipping Miranda fizzy drinks and eating chocolate (that was at the end of our street); other places you would see them sitting bored in the sun. More cars with guns and loads of Kalashnikovs everywhere.

The worst is seeing and feeling the city come to a halt. Nothing. No buying, no selling, no people running after buses. We drove home quickly. At least inside it did not feel so sad.

The ultimatum ends at four in the morning here in Baghdad – and the big question is will the attack be the same night or not? Stories about the first Gulf War are being told for the 100th time.

The Syrian border is now closed to Iraqis. They are being turned back. What is worse is that people wanting to go to Deyala, which is *in Iraq*, are being told to drive back to Baghdad. There was a rumour going around that Baghdad will be 'closed': no one goes in or out. People are being turned back at the borders of Baghdad city. There is a check-point and they will not let you pass it. There are rumours that many people have taken the path thru Deyala to go to the Iranian border. Maybe, maybe not.

If you remember, I told you a while ago that you can get fourteen satellite channels sanctioned by the state, retransmitted and decoded by receivers you have to buy from a state company. This service has been suspended. Internet will follow, I am sure.

Things on Iraqi TV today:

- An interview with the minister of interior affairs. Turned the volume down, didn't want to hear anything.
- Demonstrations in Iraqi cities.
- Yesterday the last 500 prisoners from the Iraq–Iran War were being exchanged. I can't believe they are still doing this. For fuck's sake, that war ended in 1989! Every Iraqi family can tell you a hundred heart-breaking stories about things that happen when you have thought your brother/father/son is dead and he suddenly appears after ten years.

:: **salam 12:21 AM [+]** ::

Air-raid sirens in Baghdad, but the only sounds you can here are the anti-aircraft machine-guns. Will go now.

:: **salam 5:46 AM [+]** ::

There is still nothing happening in Baghdad. We can only hear distant explosions and there still is no all-clear siren. Someone in the BBC said that the state radio has been overtaken by US broadcast. That didn't happen. The three state broadcasters still operate.

:: **salam 6:40 AM [+]** ::

Now that was really unexpected. When the sirens went on we thought we will get bombs by the ton-load dropped on us, but nothing happened, at least in the part of the city where I live. Aircraft guns could be heard for a while, but they stopped too after a while and then the all-clear siren came.

Today, in the morning, I went with my father for a ride around Baghdad and there was nothing different from yesterday. There is no curfew and cars can be seen speeding to places here and there. Shops are closed. Only some bakeries are open and of course the Baath Party Centres. There are more Baath people in the streets and they have more weapons. No army in the streets. We obviously still have electricity, phones are still working and we got phone calls from abroad, so the international lines are still working. Water is still running.

The English-speaking radio station on FM is now replaced by the Arabic language state radio programme broadcasting on the same wave length. I just say that, because last night just as the BBC was broadcasting from Baghdad (yes, we have put up the sat dish again) their news ticker (or whatever you call that red band down there) said that the Iraqi state radio has been taken over by US broadcast. We watched Saddam's speech this morning: he's got verse in it!!

:: salam 1:23 PM [+] ::

I watched al-Sahaf on al-Jazeera. He said that the US has bombed the Iraqi Satellite Channel, but while he was saying that the ISC was broadcasting and if it really did hit the ISC headquarters it would have been right in the middle of Baghdad. What was probably hit were transmitters or something. All TV stations are still working.

:: salam 4:28 PM [+] ::

The all-clear siren just went on.

The bombing would come and go in waves, nothing too heavy and not yet comparable to what was going on in 1991. All radio and TV stations are still on and while the air raid began, the Iraqi TV was showing patriotic songs and didn't even bother to inform viewers that we are under attack. At the moment they are re-airing yesterday's interview with the Minister of Interior Affairs. The sounds of the anti-aircraft artillery is still louder than the booms and bangs, which means that they are still far from where we live, but the images we saw on al-Arabiya news channel showed a building burning near my aunt's house – Hotel Pax was a good idea.

We have two safe rooms, one with 'international media' and the other with the Iraqi TV on. Everybody is waitingwaitingwaiting. Phones are still OK. We called around the city a moment ago to check on friends. Information is what they need. Iraqi TV says nothing, shows nothing. What good are patriotic songs when bombs are dropping?

Around 6.30 p.m. my uncle went out to get bread. He said that all the streets going to the main arterial roads are controlled by Baath people. Not curfew, but you have to have a reason to leave your neighbourhood – and the bakeries are, by instruction of the Party, selling only a limited amount of bread to each customer. He also says that near the main roads all the yet-unfinished houses have been taken by Party or army people.

:: **salam 10:33 PM [+]** ::

Friday, 21 March 2003

The most disturbing news today has come from al-Jazeera. They said that nine B52 bombers have left the airfield in Britain and are flying 'presumably' towards Iraq. As if they would be doing a spin around the block! Anyway, they have six hours to get here.

Last night was very quiet in Baghdad. Today, in the morning, I went out to get bread and groceries. There were no Baath Party people stopping us from leaving the area where we live – this apparently happens after the evening prayers. But they are still everywhere. The streets are empty. Only bakeries are open and some grocery shops charging four times the normal prices.

While I was buying bread a police car stopped in front of the bakery and asked the baker if they had enough flour and asked when they opened. The baker told me that they have been informed that they must open their shops and they get flour delivered to them daily. Groceries, meat and dairy products are a different story. One dairy product company (not state-owned) seems to be still operating and their cars were going around the city distributing butter, cheese and yoghurt to any open markets. Meat is not safe to buy, because you wouldn't know from where and how it got to the shops.

Anyway, we bought fresh tomatoes and zucchini for 1,000 dinar a kilo, which would normally be 250. And most amazingly the garbage car came around.

The Iraqi Satellite Channel is not broadcasting any more. The second youth TV channel (it shows Egyptian soaps in the morning and sports afterwards) also stopped transmitting. This leaves two channels: Iraq TV and Shabab (Youth) TV. They are still full of patriotic songs and useless 'news' – they love the French here. We also saw the latest Sahaf show on al-Jazeera and Iraq TV, and the most distressing Minister of Interior Affairs with his guns. Freaks. Hurling abuse at the world is the only thing left for them to do.

On BBC we are watching scenes of Iraqis surrendering. My youngest cousin was muttering 'What a shame' to himself. Yes, it is better for them to do that, but still, seeing them carrying that white flag makes something deep inside you cringe.

We sit in front of the TV with the map of Iraq on our laps, trying to figure out what is going on in the south.

:: salam 3:13 PM [+] ::

As usual, Diana comes to the rescue:

IS SALAM PAX REAL?

Please stop sending e-mails asking if I am for real. Don't believe it? Then don't read it. I am not anybody's propaganda ploy – well, except my own.

Two more hours until the B52s get to Iraq.

:: salam 6:05 PM [+] ::

Saturday, 22 March 2003

4.30 p.m. (Day 3)

Half an hour ago the oil-filled trenches were put on fire. First, watching al-Jazeera they said that these were the places that got hit by bombs from an air raid a few minutes earlier, but when I went up to the roof to take a look I saw that there were too many of them – we heard only three explosions. I took pictures of the nearest. My cousin came and told me he saw police cars standing by one and setting it on fire. Now you can see the columns of smoke all over the city.

Today we had quite a number of attacks during daytime – some without air-raid sirens. They probably just gave up on being able to be on time to sound the sirens. Last night, after wave after wave of attacks, they would sound the all-clear siren only to start another air-raid siren thirty minutes later.

The images we saw on TV last night (not Iraqi, but Jazeera/BBC/ Arabiya) were terrible. The whole city looked as if it were on fire. The only thing I could think of was 'Why does this have to happen to Baghdad?' As one of the buildings I really love went up in a huge explosion I was close to tears.

Today my father and brother went out to see what is happening in the city. They say that it does look that the hits were very precise, but when the missiles and bombs explode they wreck havoc in the neighbourhood where they fall. Houses near al-Salam Palace (where the minister Sahaf took journalists) have had all their windows broke and doors blown in and in one case a roof has caved in. I guess that is what is called 'collateral damage' and that makes it OK?

We worry about daytime bombing and the next round of attacks tonight with the added extra of the smokescreen in our skies.

Sunday, 23 March 2003

I have Internet again – will post soon.

But I must apologize to the people at industrialdeathrock.com, because the amount of traffic this blog has been getting causes their servers to go down. I am very sorry. I should have been more careful.

Looking thru my mail I see that this blog has also been causing blogspot problems. Sorry. And Blogger has been generous again with me and allowed this to go and help. Thanks. My mailbox is full because of the last two days of Internet black-out – going thru them now.

:: salam 3:24 PM [+] ::

8.30 p.m. (Day 4)

We start counting the hours from the moment one of the news channels reports that the B52s have left their airfield. It takes them around six hours to get to Iraq. On the first day of the bombing it worked precisely. Yesterday we were a bit surprised that after six hours bombs didn't start falling.

The attacks on Baghdad were much less than two days ago. We found out today in the news that the city of Tikrit got the hell bombed out of it. Today the B52s took off at 3 p.m. – in half an hour we will know whether it is Baghdad tonight or another city. Karbala was also hit last night.

Today's (and last night's) shock attacks didn't come from airplanes, but rather from the airwaves. The images al-Jazeera is broadcasting are beyond any description. First was the attack on Ansar el Islam camp in the north of Iraq. Then the images of civilian casualties in Basra city. What was most disturbing are the images from the hospitals. They are simply not prepared to deal with these things. People were lying on the floor with bandages and blood all over. If this is what 'urban warfare' is going to look like, we're in for disaster. And just now the images of US/UK prisoners and dead – we saw these on Iraqi TV earlier. This war is starting to show its ugly, ugly face to the world.

The media wars have also started. Al-Jazeera accusing the Pentagon of not showing how horrific this war is turning out to be and Rumsfeld saying that it is regrettable that some TV stations have shown the images.

Today before noon I went out with my cousin to take a look at the city. Two things: (1) the attacks are precise (2) they are attacking targets which are just too close to civilian areas in Baghdad. Look at the Salam Palace and the houses around it. Quite scary near it – and you can see windows with broken glass till very far off. At another neighbourhood I saw a very unexpected 'target': it is an officers' club of some sorts smack in the middle of [. . .] district. I guess it was not severely hit because it was still standing, but the houses around it, and this is next door and across the street, were damaged. One of them is rubble the rest are clearing away glass and rubble. A garbage car stands near the most damaged houses and helps with the cleaning up.

Generally the streets are quite busy. Lots of cars, but not many shops open. The market near our house is almost empty now. The shop owner says that all the wholesale markets in Shorjah are closed now, but the prices of vegetables and fruits have gone down to normal and are available.

While buying groceries, the woman who sells the vegetables was talking to another about the approach of American armies to Najaf city and about what is happening at Umm Qasar and Basra. If Umm Qasar is so difficult to control what will happen when they get to Baghdad? It will turn uglier and this is very worrying. People (and I bet 'allied forces') were expecting things to be much easier. There are no waving masses of people welcoming the Americans, nor are they surrendering by the thousands. People are doing what all of us are: sitting in their homes hoping that a bomb doesn't fall on them and keeping their doors shut.

The smoke columns have now encircled Baghdad, well almost. The winds blow generally to the east, which leaves the western side of Baghdad clear. But when it comes in the way of the sun it covers it totally – it is a very thick cloud. We are going to have some very dark days, literally.

We still have electricity; some areas in Baghdad don't after last night's attack. Running water and phones are working.

Yesterday many leaflets were dropped on Baghdad. While going around in the streets I got lucky, I have two. After being so unkind to the people at www.industrialdeathrock.com, I don't know whether I should post images or not.

And we have had another e-mail attack, this time I was lucky again and have copies of those, the sender is someone called blablabla@hotpop.com. I have not checked on that yet. Three of them are to army personnel and two to the general public, in which they gave us the radio frequencies we are supposed to listen to. They are calling it 'Information Radio'.

:: salam 4:41 PM [+] ::

Monday, 24 March 2003

The last two days we didn't have Internet access. I thought that was it and started what a friend called a 'pblog' – what you will read is what should have been the entries for the 22nd and 23rd.[+] Blogger and Google have created a mirror to this weblog at www.dearraed.blogspot.com, for those of you who have trouble with the underscore in the URL. There are not enough words to thank the people at Blogger for their help and support.

9.29 p.m. (Day 5)[++]

Tonight we didn't notice any news channel reporting anything from Fairford about the B52s, but then again the bombardment hasn't stopped the whole day. Last night's bombardment was very different from the nights before. It wasn't only heavier, but the sound of the bombs was different. The booms and bangs are much louder. You would hear one big bang and then followed by a number of these rumbles that would shake everything. And there are of course the series of deep dob-dob-dobs from the explosions farther away. Anyway, it is still early (it is 9.45 p.m.). Last night things got seriously going at 12, followed by bombardments at 3, 4 and 6 a.m. – each would last for 15 minutes. The air-raid sirens signalled an attack around 12 and never sounded the all-clear signal. Sleep is what you get between being woken up by the rumbles or the time you can take your eyes off the news. We hear the same news items over and over. But you can't stop yourself.

The air-raid sirens are not really that dependable. When they don't sound the all-clear after a whole hour of silence you get fidgety. The better alarm system is quite accidental. It has become a habit of the mosque muezzins (the prayer callers) to start chanting *allahu*

[+] These entries have been returned to their original order.

[++] 'The following entries, up to 1 May 2003, were first posted by Diana in May as the Internet went down in Iraq. During this time, Salam kept a diary and e-mailed the entries to Diana on 7 May.

akbar – la illaha ila allah the moment one of them hears an explosion. The next muezzin starts the moment he hears another calling, and so on. It spreads thru the city pretty fast and soon you have all the mosques doing the Takbir for five minutes or so. Very eerie, but it works well to alert everybody.

Below you see one of the e-mails we got, in English, this is loosely translated.

The subject line is 'critical info':

> **The world has united in a common cause. These countries have formed an alliance to remove the father of Qusay and his brutal regime. Qusay's father has tyrannized the sons of the Euphrates and exploited them for years and he has to be removed from power.**
>
> **The coalition forces are not here to hurt you, but they are here to help you. For your safety the coalition forces have prepared a list of instructions to keep you and your families safe. We want you to realize that these instructions are to keep you safe, even if they are, maybe, not (appropriate) [*this is a bit difficult, because even in Arabic I don't get exactly what they mean, but it sure got my attention – are they going to ask me to stand naked in the garden or something?*]. We add that we don't want to hurt innocent people.**
>
> **Please and for your safety stay away from potential targets, like TV and radio stations. Avoid travel or work near oil fields. Don't drive your cars at night. Stay away from military buildings or areas used for storage of weapons. All the mentioned are possible targets. For your safety don't be near these buildings and areas.**
>
> **For your safety stay away from coalition forces. Although they are here for not your harm [*sic*] they are trained to defend themselves and their equipment. Don't try to interfere in the operations of coalition forces. If you do these forces will not see you as civilians, but as a threat and targets too.**
>
> **Please for your safety stay away from the mentioned areas. Don't let your children play there. Please inform your family and neighbours of our message. Our aim is to remove the father of Qusay and his brutal regime.**

Then they list the frequencies for 'Information Radio'. They even plan to transmit on FM. What immediately caught my attention is the use of 'father of Qusay'. We don't say *walid Qusay* in Iraqi-Arabic, but use *abu Qusay*, and he is usually referred to as *abu Uday*, but then again Uday is obviously out of the game. No one sees him in meetings. Four of the e-mails came from a hotpop.com account, one from Lycos and another from Yahoo. I don't think they expect anyone to answer. But it is mighty interesting to see what happens if I write to one of them.

Was watching a report on al-Jazeera a while ago about Mosul and its preparations. The reporter interviewed someone from Fedayeen Saddam. He said that he is in Mosul to 'kill the Americans and kill anybody who does not fight the Americans' – there, in one short sentence, you have the whole situation in Basra, and most probably many Iraqi cities, explained. Fear is deep and trust in the people-from-Foreign is not high.

:: **salam 5:50 PM [+]** ::

Tuesday, 25 March 2003

10.05 a.m. (Day 6)

One mighty explosion at 12 midnight exactly. The raid lasted for ten minutes, then nothing. We had and are still having horrible weather. Very strong winds – hope we don't get a sandstorm.

In the oh-the-irony-of-it-all section of my life I can add the unbeliev-able bad luck that when I wanted to watch a movie, because I got sick of all the news, the only movie I had which I have not seen a hundred times is *The American President*. No joke. A friend gave me that video months ago and I never watched it. I did last night. The American 'presidential palace' looks quite good. But Michael Douglas is a sad ass president.

No Internet this morning, no Internet last night. And we just had an explosion right now (12.21). No siren, no nothing. Just one boom.

And another.

You can hear the sound of the planes. Look, this is what you hear the last two days when a huge explosion is coming: first the droning of what is, I think, a plane, then one small boom, followed by a rolling rumble that gets louder and suddenly BOOM! and the plane again.

I think this is a proper raid, because I can still hear explosions.

Laytah.

Wednesday, 26 March 2003

11.50 a.m. (Day 7)

Well, about the wishes for no sandstorm: I can tell you that the gods definitely don't listen to me. We had the fiercest ever. And it just went on and on. This morning everything was covered in sand. And not just a light film of sand, but a thick red layer. And to add to the absurdist comedy the gods are enjoying at our expense, they just drip-dropped a tiny bit of rain to make sure it all settled down, but didn't get washed away.

The skies cleared for a couple of hours around eight this morning and, as if on cue, the Americans entered the stage to make sure their role in this comedy is not forgotten and started bombing. Now we are being covered again by a new layer of sand.

My friend Stefan sent me an e-mail four days ago describing the whole thing as a Dadaist play. After the sandstorms, rain and the nonsense the news is churning out, I totally agree. Umm Qasar is under control. Umm Qasar is not safe. Basra is not a target. Basra will be attacked. Nasiriyah is under control. Nasiriyah sees heavy fighting. Would the news people please make up their mind? And the new addition to the war reporting absurdities is the 'Uprising in Basra'. From one side, the US/UK shout we were hoping/waiting for the cowardly Iraqis to stand up against their regime, and then Rumsfeld goes on TV and says 'Well . . . if they do it, we can't help them now.'

I talked to G. on the phone today. He stopped listening to the news two days ago. Don't accuse the Iraqi media of lies, because the rest are just as bad.

The reports about Iraqi TV going off-air are partially true. We don't get Iraqi TV, but other areas do. Maybe they are transmitting a weak signal or something. And we do have problems with electricity. Yesterday many areas in Baghdad had no electricity after 5 p.m., not all together, but one area after the other. Then it would come back for an hour and off again. I can't say whether this is because of the bad weather or the bombing. In some areas it was trees falling on electricity cables. Phones are still working. Unless where you live had its phoneline poles knocked off by the winds.

This morning I also met a couple of relatives from the south/south-west of Baghdad (outskirts – not within city limits). They say they have been under very heavy bombardment, probably smoothing the ground for the move on Baghdad. They also say that every now and then a couple of helicopters would hover very low to the ground. In one case, they were chased away by the landowners firing at them.

I would really like to say something about the Iraqi tribes and their farm land. There is nothing more important to them than their land. And it makes them squirm seeing the Iraqi army stationing themselves on it. This has been going on for a while, not just when the war started. They are unable to do anything about the Iraqi army taking their land, but no one minds them shooting any other people away. If the members of a tribe are living close to each other and using adjacent land plots, they will stand together to keep their area safe and that includes keeping the 'allied forces' away from their homes – and they are armed. Talking of tribes, tribe leaders are being called to different hotels in Baghdad and given big piles of Iraqi dinars.

Thursday, 27 March 2003

3.35 p.m. (Day 8)

The whole morning was spent cleaning up the mess created by the sand-rain-and-sand-again storm. Of course it was done to the beat of the bombardment. It has become the soundtrack of our lives. You wake up to the sound of bombardment; you brush your teeth to the rhythm of the anti-aircraft rat-tat-tats. Then there is the attack, which is timed exactly with our lunch-time.

Dishes are fun to do while you think about the possibility of the big window in front of you being smashed by the falling tons of explosives and so on. The first two days we would hurry inside and listen with worry, now you just sigh, look up to the sky, curse and do whatever you have to do. This, of course, is only because we live relatively far from where the action is these days. We only seriously worry about two stupid anti-aircraft guns a couple of hundred metres away. Having heard form the people who live close to 'targets' we can thank whatever gods or accidents that made us live where we do now.

Last night the bombs hit one big communication node in Baghdad. Now there are areas in Baghdad which we can't call and phones from/to abroad are pfffft . . . I have lost all hope that I will have Internet again. We drove to have a look and it is shocking, it looks as if the building has exploded from the inside. You can look thru three floors. It is just near the Saddam Tower in al-Ma'amun area. Thank God I can still call Raed. But he can't call some of his relatives. The operator just gives you the 'This number is not in use' automatic answer.

The streets are very busy. But Baghdad looks terrible with all the dirt. Everything looks like it has been camouflaged. And everybody is out in the street washing cars and driveways. A couple more stores are open and, amazingly, al-Sa'a restaurant didn't close for a single day. We all in Baghdad are very aware that we still have not seen the seriously bad days.

Basra on the other hand is in deep shit. One more word by Americans on TV about 'humanitarian aid' will make me kill my television. They have the audacity to turn us to beggars, while we will have to pay for the research and development of the weapons they are field-testing on us *and* they do it as if they are helping us with their 'humanitarian aid'.

Excuse me, but it would help much more if you would stop dropping those million-dollar bombs on us – it is cheaper for us in the long run. As much as I don't like him, al-Sahaf did say it: 'crocodile's tears', indeed. One thing made me really laugh with delight, as the Red Crescent**+** cars (Kuwaiti – and I would rather not say what I think about that) stopped at Safwan and started unloading – it got mobbed! People just went into the trucks and did the distributing themselves while the US/UK soldiers stood watching. And what did the Iraqis shout while they were around the trucks? *Bil rooh, bil daam nafdeek ya saddam!* ('We will sacrifice our souls and blood for Saddam!'). Catastrophic, and just starting.

Most worrying bit of news is something that I heard being reported by the US government: the Iraqi army is forcing all males to go into battle against Americans, threatening to kill their families if they

----
+ The equivalent of the Red Cross.

don't. Telling them that I don't feel like fighting won't help much, I guess.

Sunday, 30 March 2003

7.30 p.m. (Day 11)

Two one-person demonstrations on today's drive around the city.

One man chained to a tree just in front of the UN building in Abu Nawas. It looked rather comic. He was wearing a long leash and looked more like a dangerous person kept in check rather than an angry demonstrator. The building is empty and the glass is knocked out of most of its windows because it faces the river and many of the bombed palaces and buildings.

The other one-man effort was much more admirable – we even decided to honk our car horn and shout encouragement to him. He was standing on the intersection near al-Salhia, just beside the Ministry of Information, all alone and holding a sign saying in Arabic IRAQIS REFUSE TO TAKE ANY HUMANITARIAN AID FROM JORDANIANS AND EGYPTIANS. Right on! I wish I had the courage to stand with him, but he is standing in one of the most guarded areas at the moment. The Ministry of Information has been targeted, so was the Iraq TV building just off the road and Hizbis⁺ are all over the place. This probably means that the guy is a Hizbi himself, but still we refuse to take any aid from these countries after they have received the money for shutting up when it comes to the matter of Iraq.

The Ministry of Information is getting cleared. Yesterday there were a million people in and around it – journalists are all stationed on the building. Today all the sat dishes have gone, the tents were being dismantled and there were very few cars with the letters 'TV' taped on them with duct tape. We saw them near the Palestine-Meridian Hotel. But we were watching al-Arabiya and the BBC – they seem to have their cameras somewhere else.

Today's tour of the city was following last night's bombings of the telephone exchanges in Baghdad. Many of them have been reduced to rubble. Last night saw one of the heaviest bombings.

+ Party members.

Just after I wrote the entry in my diary all hell broke loose. There were two explosions or series of explosions, which shook the house like nothing till now. You could feel the floor shake under your feet and the walls rumble before you heard the sound of the explosions.

After seeing what has been done to the small telephone exchanges, I fear that the small one in al-Dawoodi might also be hit – and this is just too close to us. Since last night's bombings I can't call Raed too. G. can't call any of us since the first exchange was bombed. It feels like he lives in a different city. He is too far away and he can't call us.

No good news anywhere. No light at the end of the tunnel – and the American advance doesn't look that reassuring. If we had a mood barometer in the house it would read TO HELL WITH SADDAM AND MAY HE QUICKLY BE JOINED BY BUSH. No one feels like they should welcome the American army. The American government is getting as many curses as the Iraqi.

Tuesday, 1 April 2003

6.50 p.m. (Day 13)

There is one item which I have not thought I would need a big supply of: antacids. Air-raid sirens start wailing or the heavy bombs
start falling – five minutes later I go for the drawer with the antacids.
Now, every time the bombing starts my brother starts humming
Nirvana's 'Pennyroyal Tea'... But Iraqi antacids have no flavour – it
feels like you are chewing plaster of Paris.

Very heavy bombing the last two days. Although today it was very
quiet, I bet the heavy bombing will resume tonight. It is getting
heavier by the day. Somehow, when the really heavy ones fall you
feel like the house will collapse on you. Around 2 a.m. yesterday a
couple of explosions made the whole house sway – you feel the
ground beneath you move. It is said that these were the bombs that
fell on the 'Iraqi Village' – an orphanage. Well . . . we all know that
what is called the 'Iraqi Village' is actually just part of a huge area
used by the Republican Army, so no surprise it has been hit for the
second time.

We went today to the Adhamiya district to look at the damage
done there. Another small telephone exchange bombed to the
ground. The commercial buildings around it have been turned to
useless shells. It looks as if pushing one of the walls will make it
crumble and fall. And just a couple of metres further, something
which was a house is now a pile of rubble. A couple of streets
away is the Iraqi Satellite Channel. You can see the transmission
tower broken and bent, but we couldn't get near it – they had barri-
cades on all the streets leading to it. The Adhamiya is a very

dense area. These bombings must have shook the people pretty badly.

The streets are more crowded by the day and more shops are opening. Can you imagine having to stop all your work for two weeks? A huge part of the population – especially shop owners, groceries and the like – all depend on a day-by-day income. Two weeks is a lot of time with no money. Most manual labour is paid by the day and all these people have to sit at home because there is no work.

Shop owners who live near their shops are opening; banks are open (even private banks) and life goes on. Things cost double their normal price, but we are happy that you can still buy what you need from shops, because this means we can keep what we have stored for harder days which are sure to come.

If Basra is to be taken as an example, Baghdad will go thru hell. It looks as if the US/UK army will be moving on Baghdad from the west, which puts us right in their way. The Iraqi government sure sees it the same way too, because where we live is starting to look more like part of an army base.

The worst thing that could happen to you these days is having an empty or half-built house near the place you live. It will be seized by the Government. We now have Hizbis as neighbours. Two streets to the back there is something that is probably even nastier, because of the number and type of cars that are parking there during the day. The main street already looks like a battlefield because of so many trenches. Not the sandbag thingies, but proper dug trenches with people holding rocket-launchers walking around them. Great fun to be had by everyone. How on earth are they going to take Baghdad? I am afraid the areas we live in on the outer edges of Baghdad will become combat zones.

I am still trying to ignore the 24-hour, non-stop TV bombardment. News just ups the level of my paranoia. I'm living in my head-phones or watching silly videos. *Ice Age* has become a house favourite.

Wednesday, 2 April 2003

Actually too tired, scared and burnt out to write anything. Yes, we did go out again to see what was hit. Yes, everything just hurts. Conversations invariably include the sentence 'What's wrong with them? Have they gone mad?' I can't stand the TV or the lies on the news any more. No good news, wherever you look.

Baghdad is looking scarier by the minute. There are now army people everywhere. My uncle will have to move out of his house because there is going to be an anti-aircraft battery installed too close to it. The area where we live does not look too good either. We are surrounded by every sort of military outfit there is. Every school in the area is now an army or Party centre. I avoid walking in front of the school in our neighbourhood. I try the ostrich manoeuvre: see no evil = evil has vamoosed out of existence.

The news programmes drive me crazy, but they are all we are watching. I specially like the Pentagon Show: him with the distracting facial expressions and her with her loud costumes. But still, the best entertainment value you get these days is from the briefings – Iraqi and American. Al-Sahaf is outdoing himself each time he is on TV – and I know no one who can tell me what *oolouj* means. Best way to hide from the news is to live in your headphones.

Two hours ago we could hear the rumbling of the planes over us and it took them ages to pass. 'Afraid' is not the right word. Nervous, edgy – sometimes you just want to shout out at someone – angry. I wish the Iraqi *and* the American governments would stop saying they are doing this for the people. I also want to hold a NOT IN MY NAME sign.

Pachechi[+] was on all the Arabic news stations with interviews and talk shows. If it's a choice between him and Chalabi, I go for Pachechi.

Non-stop bombing. At the moment the US/UK are not winning any battle to 'win the heart and mind' of this individual. No matter which way this will go, my life will end up more difficult. You see the news

----

+ Adnan Pachechi is the elder statesman of the anti-Saddam exiles. A former foreign minister of Iraq, he is the leader of the Iraqi Democratic Group.

anchors on BBC, Jazeera and Arabiya so often you start dreaming of them – even noticing when they get a haircut and in one case on al-Jazeera, a bad dye-job.

Friday, 4 April 2003

4.30 p.m. (Day 16)

No sleep last night. If it is true that the US army is in Saddam International Airport they would be a thirty-minute drive from where Raed lives. No phones – and I am a bit too scared about driving down to his house. The phones have been a bit funny the last couple of days. It is more like a neighbourhood-wide intercom system than a telephone – you can call me if you are on the same telephone exchange.

Many people in the Jihad, Furat and along the Ameriyah Road are moving out of their homes because of fear they will end up as the front line. While we were helping one of my uncles move their water and food supplies to our place, it felt for thirty minutes like we were in the middle of no man's land. We were there just as the 'battle for the airport' started. There was another push from a more westerly direction too and this is where we got caught.

In ten minutes the whole area started moving. Cars down the road moving out of Baghdad to the west started backing up and driving down the wrong sides as fast as hell. The rumble of artillery was very close. As we drove in two cars to our place – which isn't too far away – we could see the Hizbis, army and Fedayeen taking their places around the entrances to the highway heading west out of Baghdad; and we crossed the Ghazalia Bridge minutes before they decided to block it off. Everybody was moving frantically.

Two hours later the whole city was blacked out. No electricity (at least in the western parts of Baghdad). Water stopped also, but came back a couple of hours later. Iraqis or Americans cutting the electricity off the city?

The bombardment and artillery fire went on from 6 to 9 or 10 that night and it started again at 2 past midnight with three huge explosions. Some idiots started firing their Kalashnikovs and guns and made my paranoid aunt totally believe that the American troops are in the street.

That night there was a car with a mounted gun patrolling the pitch-black streets. My uncle who lives on the main street phoned and said the street looks like a battlefield with all the troops. They have Hizbis stationed right in front of their door. In the morning they gave them tea and cake and packed their bags. They are the only people left on that street who have not moved out.

Things on TV:

- Diar al Umari and Tayseer Alluni: two al-Jazeera reporters who have been asked to leave the country (Diar is Iraqi and this might mean he's in trouble). They were probably seen with Thuraya⁺ phones and were accused of spying, which is happening a lot these days.
- Footage of people in Najaf stopping the US army from entering the shrines of Imam Ali. The troops held their guns pointed down and crouched on their knees. Their commander or something was shouting 'Smile! Smile!' and he went to shake hands with some of the Iraqis who have also sat down in front of the Americans. An Iraqi shouting into the cameras: 'City, OK! Imam Ali, No!' The question was whether to allow the Americans to enter the shrines to look for Iraqi soldiers hiding in there.
- The fight for fatwas and who-said-what concerning the invading army – and whether to fight them or assist them. All imams here and abroad are saying that no Muslim should help the invading army. But it was reported that al-Khoei⁺⁺ issued a fatwa saying that people should not 'hinder' the Americans.

Monday, 7 April 2003

11.30 a.m. (Day 19)

The Americans called it 'a show of force' and NOT the anticipated invasion of Baghdad. Well, it was definitely a great show for anyone

----

⁺ The Iraqi government banned the use of satellite phones belonging to the Thuraya satellite system (based in the United Arab Emirates), which can send a short message giving out their precise location. People were ordered to hand over their Thuraya phones so that the Government could identify 'enemy' transmissions within the country. US commanders also banned journalists accompanying its forces from using Thuraya phones.

⁺⁺ Abd al-Majid al-Khoei, a Shiite leader in Iraq, is the secretary-general of the al-Khoei Foundation, an international Islamic organization (www.al-khoei.org).

watching it from a high orbit. Added to the constant whooshes of missiles going over our heads and the following explosions, another sandstorm decided to make our life even more difficult than it already is. I mean your – ahem – boogers come out red, because of all the sand you inhale. Closing the windows is madness. It is safer to open the windows when the explosions start.

Since the day the airport was seized we have no electricity and water is not reliable. At times if you have a tap that is higher than 50 cm you won't get water from it. We turn on the generator for four hours during the day and four at night, mainly to watch the news. Today my father wanted to turn on the generator at eight in the morning, because of news of an attack on the centre of Baghdad. We sat for two hours watching the same images until Kuwait TV showed footage taken from Fox News of American soldiers in Al-Sijood Palace. Totally dumbstruck. Right after that we saw al-Sahaf denying once again what we have just seen minutes ago. He kept insisting that there are no American troops in Baghdad and for some reason kept insisting that al-Jazeera has become 'a tool of American media'. Idiot. Jazeera has been obviously very critical of the American 'invasion' (they insist on calling it that) and what does the super-smart Information Minister do? Ostracize them some more.

I have not been out of the house for the last three days. We are now fifteen people at Hotel Pax, although it is not so safe here. Everybody expects the next move to be on the west/southwest parts of Baghdad and are telling us we will *be* the front line. I can only hope when push comes to shove the Americans will not be met with too much resistance and we don't end up in the cross-fire.

Iraqi TV is still transmitting, but you need to put your antennae way up to get the signal. I did a quick search for the TV broadcast that the 'coalition forces' are supposed to be broadcasting, but couldn't find it. On the BBC a couple of hours earlier I heard Rageh Omar say that he saw a lot of people buying antennas. He said that people told him it is because they want to watch the Iraqi TV broadcast – not entirely true. Since the war started, an Iranian news channel called Al-Alam (The World) started broadcasting in Arabic and if you have a good antenna you can get it. It's actually quite informative, considering the only thing you would get otherwise is al-Sahaf on Iraqi TV telling us that the US army has been crushed and defeated.

OK, having moved around a bit and met people from different parts of Baghdad (all running away to other parts), this is what it looks like. The push did not come from the west where the airport is, but from other parts of the city, more from an east direction. Al-Saydia district was bedlam. It did become a front line. Which means Mahmudia in the suburbs of Baghdad and Latifiyah have also had it bad. There is a highway which we call the 'airport road'. This goes from Saydia all the way to the airport in one big sweep around the city and all the areas adjacent to that highway have seen fighting including Qahtan Square. Cutting thru the Karkh part of Baghdad just like that. I guess the Iraqi government will self-destruct in humiliation. Excuse me, but where are you friggin' Republican Guards?

I still worry about Raed and his family. G. will be safer now, since the attacks are now more on the fringes of the city than the central parts.

Thursday, 10 April 2003

3.00 p.m. (Day 22)

After having a house full of people for a while it feels pretty empty now. Most of the family has decided to go back to their houses. We had an amazing couple of days.

> 4 April: The Americans in the airport.
>
> 7 April: They move into Baghdad.
>
> 9 April: Troops are in Firdaws Square ('firdaws' means 'heaven') with no Iraqi military presence in the streets whatsoever. They just disappeared – puff! – into thin air. The Big Disappearing Act. Army shoes and uniforms are thrown about in every street; army cars abandoned in the middle of the road. An act of the Almighty made every army member disappear at exactly the same time, fairytale-like: '. . . and the golden carriage was turned back to a pumpkin at the stroke of twelve.'

Around 6 p.m. yesterday we turned on the electricity generator to check the news. Lo-and-behold! Holy cow in the sky! What do we see? Iraqis trying to pull down the Saddam statue in Al-Firdaws Square. That the American troops are so deep in the city was not as surprising as the bunch of people trying to pull that thing down. By now any relatives and friends have told us that they saw a lot of American soldiers in the city, even before the 9th of April. Not only the presidential palaces, but also in many residential districts. The news does not tell you everything. They quickly mentioned the Saddam Bridge, not saying that this was right beside the University of Baghdad and a stone's throw from the main presidential complex.

Yesterday we saw on TV the images of looting. The Iranian news channel (Al-Alam) showed the images and since this channel can be picked up by a normal antenna, everybody who had an electricity generator got news that the lawless phase of this attack has reached Baghdad. *Farhud* has started in Baghdad.

Farhud. The first one was the *farhud* of the Jews of Baghdad after they have been driven out of their homes – don't ask me about dates. Diana told me about that one. I never knew that the word was used to describe the plunder that happened to the homes of the Iraqi Jews: *farhud al yahood.* Then an organized *farhud* in Kuwait – that one was very systematic and state organized. Today I tell you History does not only repeat itself once, but it hits you a third time in the eye.

To see your city destroyed before your own eyes is not a pain that can be described and put to words. It turns you sour (or is that bitter?). It makes something snap in you and you lose whatever hope you had. Undone by your own hands. Close your doors. Shut your eyes. Hope the black clouds of this ugliness do not reach you. At the moment only what could be described as the Government's prosperity is being looted and destroyed – actually public property and they are only destroying what is theirs, but who is going to listen to that argument?

There have been very little attacks up till now on private property. Government stores full of cars – imported cars to be distributed as 'presents' by Saddam – have been opened and cars are being pushed out and are there for the taking. Sorry, no keys. You'll have to solve that problem by yourselves.

What I am sure of is that this could have been stopped at a snap of an American finger. The Ministry of Interior Affairs was kept off limits to the looters by the simple presence of a couple of American army cars and soldiers. Doors were shut, no one went in. At the moment we wish there was an American tank at the corner of every street.

Stories from people who do have an army tank at the corner of their street:

M. lives near one of the highways coming into Baghdad from the west. The American army has decided to put a control point at the end of their street. That was on the 7th. Some of the troops spent the night on the roof of his two-storey house. Too scared to make a sound, he kept to the ground floor and didn't move.

In the morning he heard them smashing a window and moving into the house. He ran out and made enough noise to attract their attention. He speaks good English and asked them not to do anything to his home. They said they had knocked the night before, but when no one answered they assumed no one was in. The previous night they were attacked from behind one of the cars in the street and they decided to take position on top of one of the houses. After being shot at again from behind another car, the American tanks at the end of the street just shot every car in sight to pieces and killed a number of Fedayeen types hiding in the gardens of these houses.

M. explained that the twenty or so houses were mostly empty – the people moving out as fast as they can when the news of the advance from the west came. He was lucky he didn't get shot when he came out of the house. The Americans changed their outlook post to the roof of another house.

Today he came over to my place to say 'Hi' with a white handker-chief tied to his car antenna (it is foolish these days to drive or even walk around without a piece of white cloth – too many bad 'inci-dents'). He came over and told me about the pictures he has been taking with the marines and their tanks in his street. They have been trying to be extra nice after turning the neighbourhood into a battlefield – and the troops have been invited to lunch by a couple of people there. Nice, isn't it?

Friday, 11 April 2003

(Day 23)

Last night at around 11 p.m. we turned off the electricity generator and I and my brother went upstairs. Minutes later there was a huge blast just behind our house, followed by another and another. So close, my brother started muttering 'They want *us*! They want *us*!' absurdly.

We ran downstairs hearing glass breaking and things falling on the roof. The nine of us were quickly together in the safe room, huddled together. There were twenty blasts in all and with each one we would think the next will be a direct hit at the house. This lasted for about twenty minutes. No one dared move. Someone outside was shouting 'Civilians! Civilians! Don't shoot!'

After another thirty minutes when nothing more happened, we went outside to check on the house and the neighbours. Everybody was on the street. For some reason we didn't have as much smashed glass as the people next door and there were flames and smoke coming from the next street. Too scared to walk in the open street that night, we waited until day broke. Today at seven went out to check what happened.

Three houses were turned to rubble – two more burned. Miraculously the three houses were empty. Their owners had moved out of Baghdad. The burned houses just kept burning the whole night and are still burning today. Three people got seriously injured. Couples with minor injuries were treated by people in the block. Smashed glass all over. Two cars caught fire, but miraculously did not explode. The scene is not describable. Everybody in shock. Someone from further down the street asked: 'What? Did you have Saddam as a house guest here?'

You can follow the trace of the shrapnel. It moves in a straight line across two streets. And what sort of a shell is that which blasts in mid-air and sends big bits of shrapnel all over?

My uncle lives on the main street. This is what they saw: a tank standing in front of their house, so close they could hear the soldiers speak. It started shelling in the direction of our block and went back. It is a miracle that no one was killed.

Raed came by. He and his family returned to their house today. He says that their house is a mess because all the bombing on Furat district.

Thursday, 17 April 2003

Too much has happened the last couple of days, but my head is as heavy as a lead boulder. Hay fever time. The sexual life of palm trees makes me weep.

I still can't bring myself to sleep upstairs, not that anything too serious happened after that night. But I'd rather sleep under as many walls and roofs as possible. Fist-size shrapnel gets thru the first wall, but might be stopped by the next – seen that and learned my lesson. So the million-dollar question is, of course, 'What the fuck happened?' Well, Syrian/Lebanese/Iraqi *Fedayeen* were somewhere in the area.

Fedayeen. It has become a swear word. Dirtyfilthy. And always followed by a barrage of verbal abuse. Syrian, Lebanese and, of course, Iraqi sickos who are stupid enough to believe the 'Jennah-under-martyrs-feet' rubbish. They want to die in the name of Allah, so what do they do? Do they stand in front of 'kafeer infidel aggressor'? No they don't, because they are chicken shit. They go hide in civilian districts to shoot a single useless mortar shell or a couple of Kalashnikov shots, which bounce without any effect off the armoured vehicles. But the answer they get to that single shot is a hell of mortars or whatever on all the houses in the area from where the shot came. This has been happening all over Baghdad and in many places people were not as lucky as we have been here in our block.

Sometimes you don't even know that those creepy fucks have moved into your street for the night. All over Baghdad you see the black cloth with the names of people killed during these things. It is even worse when the Americans decide to go into full battle mode on these Fedayeen, right there between the houses. I have seen what has happened in the Jamia and Adhamiya districts. One woman was too afraid to go out of her house hours after the attack, because she had pieces of one of these Fedayeen on her lawn.

Now, whenever Fedayeen are seen they are being chased away. Sometimes with rocks and stones if not guns. If you have them in your neighbourhood, you will not be able to sleep peacefully. The stupid fucks. For some reason the argument that if he wants to die, then he should do it alone and not take a whole block down with him does not hit home.

As if the crazy loonies from Syria are not enough, Iraqis are doing quite enough damage themselves.

Looters. How to explain this? Does anyone believe those who go on TV and say 'No, not-us – must be from abroad' (they mean Kuwaitis, but they are scared to say it) to explain all the looting that has been going on? How much can we blame on 'the systematic destruction of Iraq by foreigners' and how much on the Iraqis themselves? I heard the following on TV (don't know who said it): 'if Genghis Khan turned the Tigris blue from the ink of the manuscripts thrown in it, today the sky has been turned black by the smoke rising from the burning books.'

Try to rationalize and fail. The same crowd who jumped up and down shouting 'Long live Saddam!' now shouts in TV cameras 'Thank you, Mr Bush!', while carrying away whatever they can carry. Thank you, indeed. This is not the people reclaiming what is theirs, these are criminal elements on the loose.

So how clean are the hands of the US forces? Can they say 'Well, we couldn't do anything' and be let off the hook? Hell no. If I open the doors for you and watch you steal, am I not an accomplice? They did open doors. Not to freedom, but to chaos, while they kept what they wanted closed. They decided to turn a blind eye. And systematically did not show up with their tanks until all was gone and there was nothing left.

We sealed ourselves away. There is nothing a voice calling for restraint can do in front of a mob. Oh, and thanks for the tank in front of the National Museum. And the couple of soldiers on it lounging in the sun, while the looting goes on from the back door.

Since we're talking about looting, do you know who the biggest smuggler in recent years was? Arshad, Saddam's personal guard for a very long time. He even tried once to get the head of the winged minotaur in Nineveh out of the country some years ago, but it turned to a fiasco and he had to get back to the smaller things.

A Tikriti officer offered G. seventy pieces from the National Museum a couple of days after the reported looting. He and his other Tikriti friends had 150 pieces, plus other pieces from a much later period. (They turned out to be not the real thing but copies – at least that is what the Americans told G. when he showed them photos of the stolen pieces, but that is another story.)

A ten-minute walk from the National Museum, the Saddam Arts Centre is now showing white stains on its walls instead of the collection of modern art it used to have. Some of the paintings were not stolen, they were slashed or shot. Now that is a nice concept for you. Hate a painting? Go shoot it. Strange thing.

There are places where if you are seen with a weapon these days *and* shoot it, you end up dead, but it seems that if you are shooting paintings or blowing up vaults, no one minds the weapons. The worst is of course that idiot al-Zubaidi⁺ and his so-called Civil Administration. Did you see on TV those police cars and policemen he supposedly got to work? I saw them on TV too – that is about the only place I have seen them. People in districts with a strong social fabric took over the police stations themselves and were stopping and arresting the criminals. Police? Don't make me laugh.

Too depressing.

I see Raed and G. every couple of days. G., in one of his impossible and crazy adventures, ended up working with a *Guardian* team. I am just so glad that I see them again. The whole issue of American presence and Iraqi government makes us argue until we are too tired to talk. Usually, Raed ends up calling me and G. pragmatic pigs with no morals and principles. He wants to stick a sign on my forehead saying BEWARE! A PRAGMA-PIG! He talks of invading forces and foolish loonies (me) who believe that the US will help us build a democracy. But what we all agree upon is that if the Americans pull out now, we will be eaten by the crazy mullahs and

----
⁺ Muhammed Mohsen al-Zubaidi, a former Iraqi exile, proclaimed himself Baghdad's mayor in April. He was arrested by US forces and accused of exerting authority he did not have. Al-Zubaidi is associated with Ahmad Chalabi, the leader of the Iraqi National Congress.

imams. G. has decided that this might be a good time to sell our souls to the (US) Devil.

Wednesday, 23 April 2003

Yesterday I almost died of thirst in front of thirty bottles of pure water. I had 30,000 dinars in my pockets, but couldn't buy a 2,000-dinar bottle. (2,000 in itself is a crime – you used to get four bottles for that price, but what to do, the war and all?) 30,000 dinars in 10,000 bills, which now have the stigma of being stolen on them. There is no way to plead and swear on all that is holy that these are pre-invasion 10,000 bills.

The story goes as follows: the money-printing works have been looted just like everything else. Al-Jazeera showed the wrecked 10,000-bill press and showed an Iraqi who was not identified (he could be one of the looters for all we knew), who said that printed but unnumbered 10,000 bills were stolen, as well as the printing templates (or whatever they are called – we call them *kalisha*). Paper and the shiny stripes too. Al-Jazeera said that what is on the market now are the printed bills with counterfeit numbers on them. Havoc rules the street. Your 10,000 bills are not accepted at stores. And there are people who buy your 10,000 for 8,000 dinar. And what does Mr Zubaidi, who knows fuck-all, say? His 'financial adviser' – another self-appointed ex-thief befriended with Al-Chalabi – told him that the Iraqi Central Bank is able to cover the money, so it should not be a problem. Ho-humbug. Who are you to say anything about the Central Bank?

A little aside here, before I get back to the 10,000 bills. Do you know what the new sceptre and crown of this state is? A Thuraya phone and an Iraqi National Conference flag – Chalabi's people. Makes you wonder. Anyway, anything al-Zubaidi says can be taken with a ton of salt. We be listenin' to what the Americans say. I would rather look at the puppet-master than the puppet.

Back home I find uncle M., who is a banker type, actually the executive director of a bank. After telling him what happened, he says that they have been having meetings with the 'puppet-masters' and they are going to issue a statement concerning the 10,000 bill problem. But this will be more directed at the banks until there is a way to get this to the street level, because there is still no TV or radio *and* no electricity. He kept banging on about those vultures who are trying to make a quick dinar and making matters worse. Uncle M., riding his high moral horse and galloping off to the horizon. I actually only wanted to know what to do with my 10,000 bills. Burn them? Make paper airplanes? Shred to confetti? He gave me the answer I wanted to hear: 'Give them to me. I will get you 250-dinar bills tomorrow.' He was annoyed with me, but I was only too happy to have banker people in the family.

The last couple of days I have been having the vilest thoughts about Chalabi, Zubaidi *et al*. I can't stop myself muttering filthybad things about them whenever one of these names gets mentioned. Oh, and the hideous flag they have.

Who gave them permission to camp at the grounds of the Mansour Social Club *and* the Iraqi Hunting Club. What am I supposed to do with my membership? Where do I find another big indoor swimming pool? No, seriously. What is it with these foreign political parties who have suddenly invaded Baghdad? Do they have no respect for public property? Or since it is the 'season of the loot' they think they can just camp out wherever they like and – ahem – 'liberate' public buildings. PUK+ at the National Engineering Consultants' building. KDP++ at the Mukhabarat building in Mansour. INC+++ taking an army conscription centre. Islamic Dawa at the children's public library. Another Islamic-something taking a bank. Out! Out! Out! Liberate your own backyard. You have no right to sit in these buildings.

There is only one 'liberated' building I did find worth applauding, because it was only symbolic. On the side entrance to the Central Mukhabarat building in Harthiya you will find written in red spray-paint *The Iraqi Communist Party*. In a twisted, macabre upside-down way this is the centre of the Iraqi Commies. These buildings have been filled with Iraqi Communist Party members who were imprisoned, tortured and killed there.

The 'Iraqi Media Network' started broadcasting yesterday. Nothing

---

+ The Patriotic Union of Kurdistan.
++ The Kurdistan Democratic Party.
+++ The Iraqi National Congress.

to go crazy about. They are apparently recording one single hour and broadcasting it for 24 hours. They are using it for announcements by the coalition forces mainly, beside the coalition radio station 'Information Radio'. They have brought Ahmad al-Rikabi from Radio Free Iraq/Radio Free Europe. Yesterday also, the Iraqi media people (journalists, TV and radio people) were demonstrating in front of the Meridian Hotel asking for their jobs back. Wait in line! We all are.

During the last couple of weeks in this big media festival called 'The Iraq War', the irony is that there is not a single Iraqi voice.

A conversation overheard by G. while in the Meridian Hotel (the Iraqi media centre):

Female Journalist 1: Oh honey, how *are* you? I haven't seen you for ages.

Female Journalist 2: I think the last time was in Kabul.

Female Journalist 1: Blah blah blah.

Female Journalist 2: Blah blah blah.

Female Journalist 1: Have to run now, see you in Pyongyang then, eh?

Female Journalist 2: Absolutely.

Iraq is taken out of the headlines. The search for the next conflict is on. Maybe if it turns out to be Syria the news networks won't have to pay too much in travel costs.

Saturday, 26 April 2003

G. and I went to the Meridian to do an errand. The day we went to the Meridian most of the media was checking out – if you are staying for long periods it makes more sense to get a house for yourself.

After we left the hotel we stood for a while looking at a 'demonstration' in front of the Meridian. Iraqi army officers were doing something in the Alwiyah Club building and everybody was selling photocopied papers which are supposed to be job applications or something.

A whole market has emerged right there in front of the two hotels, the Meridian and the Sheraton. Thuraya (www.thuraya.com) phone-owners standing in front of their cars offering you phone calls abroad for $5 a minute (it actually costs less than a dollar). Photocopy shops to make copies of whatever the coalition is throwing at the people today. People with foldable chairs and cardboard boxes in front of them offering to exchange your dollars. No idea why the cardboard box – maybe to make it look like an office. Cigarette vendors, too, and various sandwiches are on offer, but they don't look too safe to eat. The atmosphere is like a festival. We only needed live music and a beer stand.

Whatever . . .

G. had a falafel sandwich and we drank *ZamZam Cola*. Baghdad is flooded with *ZamZam Cola* – named after the 'holy' well in Mecca. It's an Iranian product and tastes too sweet. But since it is called *ZamZam* it must have some divine qualities. I have been drinking *ZamZam Cola* for a while now. I am expecting to grow angel wings any day.

> May 2003

Thursday, 1 May 2003

May Day. Workers of the world unite. The Iraqi Communist Party and the Iraqi Communist *Workers'* Party are covering a lot of walls with red posters. I have not heard that Nadia Abdul Majeed of the Communist Workers' Party is in Baghdad. I am still offering to volunteer, if they do some cosmetic changes to their name. They have their hearts in the right place, unlike most other parties who have their hearts near their wallets. But 'Communist'? I will look like a Communards fan if I start wearing red stars and buttons with the sickle-and-hammer thing. Nothing against Mr Somerville,[+] but I'm past that phase and no one could ever sing along to his falsetto anyway.

Sa'ad al-Bazaz and his newspaper *Az zaman* (www.azzaman.net) have launched their attack on Baghdad. It is quite good compared to the ~~leaflets~~ newspapers the various parties are printing and distributing. *Az zaman* looks like it has big money behind it and there is very little advertising. It has a very good culture section called *Alef yaa* (www.alefyaa.com). But people are reading everything they get their hands on.

With the exception of a newspaper called *New Iraq* – a weekly at the moment because it is privately funded by a number of Iraqi journalists – the rest of them are tripe. They could be one of the old Iraqi papers: a picture of the leader of X party 'among his people', news of the great achievements of that party. Blah blah blah. Good for the peanut vendors on the street – makes good paper cones.

[+] Jimmy Somerville, the singer in the 1980s band The Communards.

Sa'ad al-Bazaz is an example of how it is nonsense to say 'Throw all the Baathists out!' He was the editor of one of the regime's big newspapers. He left the country on a mission to write a book about Saddam or something like that and never came back. If you are going to 'de-Baathify' (as Chalabi is calling it), then I guess you will have to throw al-Bazaz out, but that would be a mistake. The newspaper coming out in his name shows that he might be helpful in licking Iraqi media into shape. And there are many like him. There are, of course, unforgivable atrocities committed by a number of Baathists, but there is no need to put every single Iraqi who was one under house arrest. That would mean we would have no teachers in schools, no professors in universities and everybody who worked in a state company will be made to quit his job.

G. would kill me for saying this. He is still waiting for the masses to rise. He believes in something he calls 'the Red Mullahs'. The Islamic Dawa Party and the Communist Party should be in a coalition, he says. Tsk tsk, this coming from a Christian. Maybe I should give *him* my Communards tapes?

The people are doing their own filtering anyway. After many have been called to go back to their jobs, some are refusing to work under certain people whom they know are too Baathist to tolerate now. A friend was telling me when the bus came to take him to his workplace, one of them turned around to one of the Baathists who worked there telling him that if he is coming in the bus he will have shoes thrown at him and kicked out of it. There were other Baath Party members on the bus, but everybody knows who was the bad apple. Generalizations, like al-Chalabi's de-Baathification plans, don't solve problems.

There are stories in southern governorates of Baathists making 'pre-emptive strikes' at people they are scared might come and kill them.

And the looting goes on. A week ago the hottest items to steal were number plates from cars. People started putting them *inside* the car to make sure they don't get stolen. You see, after a bazillion cars were stolen, many without any number plates on them, they had to find a way to make them look legal, because some cars were being stopped in the street if they didn't have a number. There are three different number plates you can get. The worst are the plates stolen from the number-plate factory, because there is no way you can get papers for that – they simply do not exist, but they are cheap at only 15,000 dinars (exchange rate these days is 2,000 dinars for one US dollar). The second best are the number plates found for sale on the street, stolen from cars parked right there, but with no papers. The best are number plates with all the necessary papers. You'll pay for that quite a bit, and if you are lucky you will find papers for a car just like the one you have 'liberated' – no one looks at things like chassis numbers anyway.

But that is old now. If you are an enterprising looter, you go to the weapons factories around Baghdad. The huge empty cannon shells you find there are very desirable items – the metal is melted and used. And there is an endless supply of these shells. There are big battles being raged around the *qa'qah* (al qa3qa3) factory every night to control it. There are now around thirty dead people and a number of wounded. The coalition forces are enjoying the scene and keeping their distance.

They are like that in most of the cases. They sit looking a bit bored, watching the looting. Sometimes, if it is not too troublesome, they will go check on what is happening – if you jump in front of their tanks shouting 'Ali Baba! Ali Baba!' Cute, isn't it? We have found common ground in the stories of *The Thousand and One Nights*. Everybody knows the story of Ali Baba and the forty thieves, but not everybody speaks English. So if you are lucky the Americans will come to check what Ali Baba is doing. Sometimes they care, sometimes they don't.

A couple of days ago I was walking down al-Rasheed Street when the Americans seemed to be interested in an 'Ali Baba' situation – a bit too interested. Two small armoured vehicles were coming down the street with a couple of soldiers running after them with their guns pointed to the front. The gods, enjoying another one of their sick jokes, put me right in front of the door of the building they were checking at the exact moment they decide to go in. The two cars come in real fast, one in front, one behind me. The soldiers start running faster. I almost pee in my pants with my hands up saying 'Don't shoot! Don't shoot!' They didn't.

The next day I walk by the same building, the entrance looks burned. Almost a statistic.

G. also had such a near-death experience while standing near a barbed wire fence somewhere in the north. He was standing there when a man came out of a car, wearing a *dishdasha* with his hands in his pockets and walking towards the fence. A soldier standing near G. starts humming to himself 'Get your hands out of your pockets' in a sing-song way and pointed his gun at the man. Thankfully, the man decides to stop scratching his balls and starts scratching his nose. Gun goes down.

Someone apparently decided that it was time the US army does some public relations work and is sending the soldiers around the city for a walk-and-talk mission. Ameriyah Road, a couple of days ago, had four tanks parked along it and soldiers in groups of five strolling along, talking to shop owners and grocers. Flak-jacket and guns in front of them, but they were trying to look amiable. Laughing and asking for prices of stuff. One of them was holding a huge sack full of candy and the kids were on him like anything. Bought bottles of *Pepsi* and were offered Iraqi bread. This scene I saw later in other places.

Some of the most dangerous places to be at these days are gas stations – too many accidents. And with all the long lines and people waiting their turn the number of casualties is high. I generally avoid crowds these days. No one knows what might happen.

Wednesday, 7 May 2003

A Post from Baghdad Station

Note: Salam Pax sent me this+ in a Word attachment earlier today. After weeks of silence, everything's happening at once: yesterday I received an e-mail from his cousin with Salam's satellite phone number. I called it. Salam's father decided to play grumpy patriarch and told me to call back in 'two minutes', which I did. Salam sounds fine. We discussed as many things as we could in a short amount of time. Without further ado, I present his latest posts. Please excuse any formatting weirdnesses. I've already been warned not to blog at work, so can't take the time to clean anything up.

+ This refers to the last fifteen entries, from 24 March to 1 May.

PS from Diana: *Before we concluded, I said, 'Salam, I just want to say one thing.' And I said, 'Fuck Saddam Hussein!' as loud as I could without disturbing the neighbours. Now, I've got nothing personal against the guy, in fact, it is hard for me to hate him as he strongly resembles my late, dear uncle (I tell you, he could be one of those doubles, except he's dead), but I just wanted to make a point. Which is: now we can say those things without fear of getting relatives or friends dragged off and killed. And Salam said, 'Everybody on the street is saying this like a mantra, "Fuck Saddam! Fuck Saddam! Fuck Saddam . . ."' (Well, maybe Salam didn't use the word 'mantra', but you get the point.) I think we can't possibly understand what it's like to be Iraqi. It must be like being in a root cellar for thirty-five years, and now you are stumbling around in the light, blinking your eyes, wondering if what you see is real, or a dream.*
-- Diana Moon

If you are reading this it means that things have gone as I hope and either Diana or my cousin has posted to the blog. One of the funniest things was talking to my boss in Beirut after the war (Thuraya should make an ad saying: 'Operation Iraqi Freedom – brought to you in association with Thuraya phones') and him telling me that someone called Diana Moon is bugging us about a certain Salam Pax. I can't even remember telling her where I work. Diana, you *are* the wise oracle of Gotham.

Today while going thru Karada Street I saw a sign saying SEND AND RECEIVE E-MAIL. AFFORDABLE PRICES. I am checking out the place tomorrow. If the price really is affordable, I might be able to update the blog every week or two.

Let me tell you one thing first. War sucks big time. Don't let yourself ever be talked into having one waged in the name of your freedom. Somehow, when the bombs start dropping or you hear the sound of machine-guns at the end of your street, you don't think about your 'imminent liberation' any more.

But I am sounding now like the taxi-drivers I have fights with whenever I get into one.

Besides asking for outrageous fares (you can't blame them: gas prices have gone up ten times, *if* you can get it), they start grumbling and mumbling and at a point they would say something like 'Well, it wasn't like the mess it is now when we had Saddam.' This is usually my cue for going into rage-mode. We Iraqis seem to have very short memories or we simply block the bad times out. I ask them how long it took for us to get the electricity back again after the last war? Two years until things got to what they are now, after two months of war. I ask them how was the water? Bad. Gas for car? Non-existent. Work? Lots of sitting in street tea-shops. And how did everything get back? Hussein Kamel✦ used to literally beat and whip people to do the impossible task of rebuilding.

Then the question that would shut them up: 'So, dear Mr Taxi-Driver, would you like to have your Saddam back? Aren't we just really glad that we can now at least have hope for a new Iraq? Or are we Iraqis just a bunch of impatient fools who do nothing better than grumble and whine? Patience, you have waited thirty-five years for days like these, so get to working instead of whining.' End of conversation.

The truth is, if it weren't for intervention this would never have happened. When we were watching the Saddam statue being pulled down, one of my aunts was saying that she never thought she would see this day during her lifetime.

BUT . . .

War. No matter what the outcome is, these things leave a trail of destruction behind them. There were days when the Red Crescent was begging for volunteers to help take the bodies of dead people off the city street and bury them properly. The hospital grounds have been turned to burial grounds. When the electricity went out and there was no way the bodies can be kept until someone comes and identifies.

I confess to the sin of being an escapist. When reality hurts, I block it out – unless it comes right up to me and knocks me cold. My mother, after going out once after Baghdad was taken by the US

✦ Hussein Kamel, the former director of Iraq's Military Industrialization Organization (in charge of Iraq's weapons programme), defected to Jordan on 7 August 1995. He provided documents about Iraq's past weapons programmes to UNSCOM. He returned to Iraq and was assassinated on 23 February 1996.

army, decided she is not going out again – not until I promise it looks kind of normal and OK. So I guess the Ostrich manoeuvre runs in the family.

Things *are* looking kind of OK these days. Life has a way of moving on. Your senses are numbed, things stop shocking you. If there is one thing you should believe in, it is that life will find a way to push on. Humans are adaptable. That is the only way to explain how such a foolish species has kept itself on this planet without wiping itself out. Humans are very adaptable, physically and emotionally.

And I also confess that I am going thru massive Internet withdrawal symptoms.

So here are what should have been fifteen entries to the blog, for whatever it is worth.✝

Friday, 9 May 2003

Just a quickie, because Raed will kill me if I will be late.

I now not only have access to someone with access to e-mail, but I also have access to a phone. So I got a chance to talk to Diana. She said I sounded British. And Stefan also called. If you have been reading the blog for a while you will know that he is the person I have shared a flat with for four years in Vienna. He said he will call again today and we will have more time to talk about the blog and all. I am sure some of this 'talk' will end up published somewhere in Austria, because he has been working with the Austrian News Agency. If you want to know more you will have to ask him since I have no idea what he does with these things. I still don't know what he did with that e-mail interview we did a couple of weeks before the war started.

Yesterday, after e-mailing the huge entry to Diana, I took a walk down Karada and saw three tanks parked in front of an ice-cream shop. Pretty surreal. And later, at night, four of the soldiers stationed in al-Ameriyah Street were walking back holding these kerosene lights we call *laleh*. They have bought them from the shop

----
✝ These entries have now been returned to their chronological sequence.

down the street because their generator broke down or something. Nightwatch done in very romantic light.

Laytah.

:: salam 5:57 AM [+] ::

Five US dollars for a single hour of browsing! Talk about someone milking it. I wonder if they would let me pay for only half an hour?

I am not complaining. I would not have believed anyone who would have told me a week ago that I will be able to browse at all. There are more of these centres popping up here and there, so the prices will go down. Besides, I have heard today that a NGO called Communication sans frontiers has arrived in Iraq and will help.

They will probably be doing what the Red Cross is doing: a centre in Baghdad and a team moving around Iraq. The Red Cross has been moving its phone service (if you can call it that) around Baghdad. Two days for each district and they depend on word of mouth to spread the news. Usually they end up with huge lines and waiting lists, but everybody is grateful.

Many people have no way of telling their relatives abroad how they are doing. A couple of Arabic TV stations (mainly al-Jazeera) have been putting their cameras in the street and allowing people to send regards to their relatives abroad – tell them they are OK, hoping they are watching at the time. So what the Red Cross has been doing, and I think what Communication sans frontiers would ulti-mately be doing, is much appreciated. The only way to communi-cate with the world otherwise is to go buy a Thuraya phone – very expensive by any standard ($700! Down from $1,500 two weeks ago – that's not counting the call-charges). I don't know how long it will take until a network can be put up. Since the one we had is now reduced to rubble.

I have made a very un-Salam decision today. I let Raed talk me into going along with him on his next two-day trip to the south. I am a bit of a coward. I am not dealing too well with all the bad things around me in Baghdad. I move thru the city with a wince. And what he has been telling me about his trip last week made me just want to crawl deeper into my cocoon.

So what is Raed up to? Raed has been working for the last two weeks with a small outfit that is calling itself Campaign for Innocent Victims in Conflict (CIVIC) – they thought about the acronym before the name, didn't they? They are a very small team of volunteers and almost-volunteers (I mean, they are getting paid much less than their effort deserves) who are going around residential districts that have seen military action with these forms and trying to get as much information as they can about civilian deaths and injuries. They are also collecting hospital records in order to come to an estimation of the number of civilian casualties. Until now they have around 5,000 injuries and deaths in Baghdad and they are starting to form teams in other Iraqi cities.

This is what he wants to drag me into. We will go to Karbala, Samawah, Nasiriyah, then Basra. And back thru Kut. These names should be familiar. They have been thru quite a bit during the war. Raed has already been to these places (with the exception of Kut) and has put together teams there. In Samaweh we will meet one of our university friends and spend the night at his place, because our driver, Abu-Saif, does not like the idea of arriving in Nasiriyah late and spending the night there. He also says that the only unsafe bit of the trip will be the way thru Kut. Did you know we have a *hizbullah* now in Iraq? Right there in Kut an Amarah. (Do you know what *hizbullah* means? It means 'God's faction', 'Allah's party'.) This *hizbullah* is calling itself *hizbullah al iraqi* and is anti-Iranian. We will be going thru *hizbullah* territory and this makes Abu-Saif uneasy. We'll see. We will leave early Saturday and should be back on Monday. Wish us a safe trip.

Prices of weapons on the market have been going up. At one point you could get a hand grenade for 500 dinars – that's a quarter of a dollar. A Kalashnikov for $200 and a brand new Uzi for a bit more. These are on display on the roads in the Baghdad-al-Jadeeda and al-Baya districts, but the cheapest can be found in the Thawra ('Revolution') district. (At least it used to be called Thawra under Saddam. Now they are calling it al-Sadir district.) It is like a militarized zone in Thawra. If you don't live there you better not go.

The street markets look like something out of a William Gibson novel. Heaps of cheap RAM (stolen of course) is being sold beside broken monitors and falafel stands – and weapons are all available.

Fights break out just like that and knives come out from nowhere – knives just bought five minutes ago. There are army sighting thingies – weird-looking things with lenses. And people selling you computer cases who tell you they are electric warmers, never having seen a computer case before.

Really, truly surreal. Software CDs, movie CDs and cheap porn. And a set of five CDs called *The Crimes of Saddam*. It has things from Halabja,* the footage they taped during 1991 while squishing the uprising after the war and other stuff about Uday. There is a whole CD about Uday. Have not seen any of them yet. They say there is some gruesome footage on them, but the Uday CD is not as juicy as you'd think.

Back to the weapons. The prices have been going up because they are being bought from the market in big quantities. One of the very few bright ideas our new American administration has been having was if the looters want money for the stolen weapons, let's pay them for bringing them to us. Outside Baghdad it is said people are being paid a fixed price for each piece of weaponry they bring in. In Baghdad it is being bought off the market at street prices. But still no one is going into the Thawra district.

American civil administration in Iraq is having a shortage of Bright Ideas. I keep wondering what happened to the months of 'preparation' for a 'post-Saddam' Iraq. What happened to all these 100-page reports? Where is that Dick Cheney report? Why is every single issue treated like they have never thought it would come up? What's with the juggling of people and ideas about how to form that 'interim government'? Why does it feel like they are using the let's-try-this, let's-try-that strategy? Trial and error on a whole country?

The various bodies that have been installed here don't seem to have much co-ordination between them. We all need to feel that big sure and confident strides forward are being taken. It is not like this at all. And how about stopping empty, pointless gestures and focusing on things that are real problems? Can anyone tell me what the

---

+ Iraqi aircraft shelled the Kurdish city of Halabja with chemical weapons on 16 March 1988, leaving 5,000 dead and 7,000 injured. The attack took place during the Iran–Iraq War, when Iraq enjoyed the support of the West against Iran. After Gulf War I, an uprising in Halabja was brutally suppressed by the Iraqi government.

return of children to schools really means? Other than it makes nice six o'clock news footage.

Schools have been looted. There are schools that have cluster bombs thrown in them when Fedayeen were still there. No one bothered to clean that mess up before issuing the call on 'Information Radio' that all students should go back to schools. How about clearing the mess created by the sudden disappearing of the ration distribution centres? How about getting the hospitals back in shape? How about making it safe to walk in the street?

I mean, there are a million more pressing issues for these committees meeting daily than getting children back to unsafe schools.

Yes, yes. I know. Patience. God needed seven days to finish his work and all that.

Living in my headphones. The best place to be these days.

:: salam 11:47 AM [+] ::

I am going thru my e-mail and cleaning up the boxes. You can stop bothering Diana with mail. I just hope she is not too upset with me.

:: salam 12:06 PM [+] ::

Monday, 19 May 2003

The people at Electronic Iraq+ and al-Muajaha++ kindly agreed to host the images for this post and we will put up the post on their site too. I have warned them that I have a lot of images and, as the Arabic saying goes, *Wa qad u'thira man anthar* ('Don't blame someone who has already given you a warning'). I really didn't have any other choice, the guys at the Internet place wanted to charge 66,000 dinars for uploading 1.2 megs of images. That's around $50 by today's rate. You should see how people react when they tell them how much they charge. Because of the rise in the value of the dinar, even richrich people from Foreign find them expensive and start bartering. We buy Internet time like we buy tomatoes now:

+ www.electroniciraq.net.
++ www.almuajaha.com.

'Look, if I spend an extra half hour, will the rate go down 3,000 dinars?'

Three days in the south of Iraq. A quick run from Baghdad to Basra and back. Since I am only tagging along, I didn't really have a say on where to go and what to see. Raed had to check on the CIVIC teams (you can check the site, iraqvictimsfund.org – but I have been told by Marla+ that it is not very informative at the moment). Raed has teams in a couple of cities and had to form new teams in others. The only place which has some sort of an administrative structure left in Iraq after the chaos are hospitals. We meet the teams in various hospitals and medical centres.

Lots of pictures to take and lots of people to talk to. We were moving to the south at the same time as al-Hakiem (the leader of the SCIRI)++ was making his trip to Baghdad. We crossed paths on his way towards Samawah. In Basra I discovered the *best* ice-cream place in all of Iraq – really the best and so cheap. I was also given 'the finger' by a British soldier while trying to take pictures of the burned-down Basra (ex)Sheraton Hotel. That is one picture I am really sad that it didn't turn out good. It would have been great: half of him hanging out of a military car giving me the finger. Now that's a souvenir to bring back from Basra.

*

The Saddam Hospital in Najaf has now changed to the Sadir Hospital. One icon goes, another comes. I came back from the trip to Basra seriously worrying that we might become an Iran-clone. If anyone went to the streets now and decided to hold elections we will end up with something that is scarier than Khomeini's Iran.

What looked like a gay parade on wheels with lots of pink flags turned out to be al-Hakiem's welcoming committee near Samawah. Don't ask me why the pink flags – I couldn't figure that one out. The colour of the SCIRI flag is red, but all you see are pink flags.

+ Marla Ruzicka, the project co-ordinator, who worked with Global Exchange to pressure the US government to set up a fund for Afghan families harmed in Operation Enduring Freedom.
++ Muhammed Said Bakir al-Hakiem is the leader of the Supreme Council for Islamic Revolution in Iraq (SCIRI).

Saw some graffiti in English on a wall: CITIZENS OF THE NOBLE HOME NAJAF DEMAND FOR THE RETURN OF THEIR DEVOTED SON, HIS EMINENCE, GOD'S GREAT MIRACLE, MUHAMED BAKER AL-HAKIEM. G. was in Najaf while 'God's great miracle' made his speech and cried. Very good theatrical effects. You see, al-Hakiem is being accused of not being here and going thru what other Shia parties have gone thru (i.e. the Islamic Dawa Party and the people around al-Sadr). His tears got the desired effect from the crowds, apparently. Unfortunately, Raed was in too much of a hurry to take time and see what Najaf was like at the arrival of 'God's great miracle'.

*

One of the biggest surprises when we got to Karbala was that Raed has a girl on his CIVIC team there. She has sent her brother to ask if it was OK for a woman to join. She keeps a notebook for the cases she wants CIVIC to try to help as fast as they can. She told us about um-Khudair, who is a thirty-year-old mother with six children. Her husband was fifty, but he died when their house was bombed. The house has been destroyed. Um-Khudair and her six children now live in one room in a *khan* (these are hotel-like buildings managed by mosques). She is pregnant as well. Sabah, the girl on the CIVIC team, tried to make Raed promise that he will do something, but he can't promise anything really. There is nothing worse than giving people false hope in situations like these and we remind the team not to give the people they interview any promises. CIVIC at the moment can only collect information and, in extreme cases, forward the info to an organization that has the funds and capability to help.

After the meeting they insist on going to the city and buy us drinks (juice). Sabah does not join us, but she asks Raed if she could take a picture with him.

I am not so sure about the juice place, so we decide on canned fizzy drinks. *Kufa-Cola*. Iraqi Shia soft drinks (Kufa is a city with an important Shia mosque). How good is that? I bet 'God's great miracle', al-Hakiem, *only* drinks *Kufa-Cola*.

While sipping on our blessed cokes, Riyadh, one of the older volunteers, tells us about an army training camp where families have taken shelter after their houses were bombed or couldn't pay the rent the last two months, when the country came to a standstill. Since this is one of the things CIVIC is looking into, Raed decides to take a look.

*

At the camp we get to meet Saif al-Deen, a huge name for a little kid who has a problem with 'S's (if you ask him, he'll tell you his name is 'Thaif') and Ibrahim with his little brother. Saif al-Deen (Sword of the Faith) and his family had to move to the army training camp when his father, a soldier in the Iraqi army, couldn't pay the rent for last two months: $10 per month.

In total there are eight families at the camp. They say they have been moved from other places. They have squatted within the city, until they got to this army centre in the outskirts. When we asked who moved them out of the places they were in, they said it was usually the new political parties. These buildings were NOT given to these parties by the 'coalition forces'. The Americans here have decided to not look at that situation for now. I think that when ministries and other public institutions start functioning again, they will ask for their property back. I can't see why the Dawa Party should take the place of a public library. Anyway, both the newly homeless and the parties are competing to occupy public buildings.

The problem in the one we went to was that this training centre is full of ammunition. And one unexploded thingy that has been fired at the camp from a helicopter. The kids run around showing us where the grenades and other stuff lies. There is no use putting up the warnings (given to organizations by the coalition forces to put at places where there are unexploded objects – mainly cluster bombs), because no one in this place can read or write. The only thing to do is to ask the families that are living near the back of the camp to move away from the areas where the ammunition is. They tell us that this is just training ammunition and not dangerous. And they won't move out of this place, because they have nowhere else to go.

We also go take a look at a neighbourhood where the Iraqi army tried to hide armoured vehicles, which later got attacked by missiles from helicopters. In many cases the soldiers and the civilians were warned by dropping leaflets; in some cases that didn't happen. No one got injured here, because they had left the area after the Iraqi army positioned four vehicles in the streets, but a couple of houses got badly damaged. The families moved back and repaired what could be repaired.

Enough about Karbala. Next stop Najaf, then Diwaniya.

*

We get to Saddam General Hospital in Diwaniya after we pass thru the Shamia area. Scenes of typical Iraqi rural areas: mud houses and palm trees. Then suddenly you see the Shamia check-point.

The Shamia medical centre saw forty-four civilian deaths in one single night – all made the same mistake of getting near the check-point on a day when the US army was having a bit of a mood. The people who live there told us that it was one of the sandstorm days. Everything that approached the check-point was shot at without any discrimination. One of the cars was carrying the casket of a dead woman to the cemetery. All four passengers died.

It was bad during these days, not for the civilians only but for the 'coalition forces'. These were days when the number of suicide attacks was increasing and after the woman who killed a number of American soldiers in one of these attacks, they changed the rules of engagement (is that what it's called?). There was no way an Iraqi could approach an area where US troops where stationed without risking a 50/50 chance of being shot at because your pockets looked funny.

At Diwaniya Hospital, Raed had to look around for people who would want to volunteer, and I looked around too.

The US army was helping the hospital bring back X-ray machines and other stuff that was stored elsewhere, to make sure it didn't get looted. Afterwards, they stood around for a while, took pictures and let the kids poke their big biceps. 'Strong mister.'

Throughout the south, in all the hospitals we have been to, there was military presence. In Kut there were FIF (Free Iraqi Forces – Chalabi's militia): people wearing exact same uniforms as the Americans, but with little badges saying FIF. Not high on my top five list. Yes, I don't like Chalabi. Go sue me.

Having military there makes everybody feel safer, to the point where, in Basra, because the main general hospital and the college of medicine are in the same compound, the British forces are making the area safe enough for that college to be the only one with regular attendance and classes. A couple of metres away, someone was stacking 'humanitarian aid' boxes on a cart and pushing it out of the hospital.

There is absolutely no distribution method. The aid that is coming in gets taken by whomever and sold on the market. You could buy the whole box for 16,000 dinars (a bit more than $16 by today's rate). Or you can buy only the things you like. Everybody is buying the chocolates and leaving the sugar and rice. This scene was repeated everywhere – in Basra these boxes were on the street. Did I mention these boxes were from Kuwait? There are others from Emirates and Saudi Arabia on the market. Water gets sold separately: 1,000 dinars per bottle. A family in need was supposed to get one box and twelve bottles of water.

Diwaniya wasn't so great. For some reason it was difficult to find the enthusiasm I have seen in Karbala and Najaf. Anyway, a CIVIC team was formed. Next stop Samawah, where we will spend the night.

*

While checking on the team in Samawah, one of the volunteers told us that they were not able to go around the city, because everybody was too distressed about the mass graves found at the edge of the city. Many who were buried there were from Samawah. At least they can be thankful that the buried had their ID cards with them and could be identified. All over the city you could see photocopied photos of the executed.

Gruesome fact: during the uprising after the first Gulf War, Saddam's henchmen, in order to move quickly, would put people in trucks and move them to the edge of the city and bury them alive. These are the mass graves where you'll find people still have their IDs: fully dressed, only with their hands tied. In every shop window, on every wall, the faces look back at you. This was not one of the big mass graves found. There were around fifty bodies.

Too tired to want to take a walk thru the city. Next day is Nasiriyah, a very big number of casualties are expected there and CIVIC still has no team there.

*

The official number in Nasiriyah (i.e. coming from hospitals and medical centres in the area) is about 1,000 civilian deaths and 3,000 injuries. Nasiriyah is not that big. With these numbers it must have seen very bad days. We go fast to the Nasiriyah Hospital and get a team together. To our amazement we have a lot of girls wanting to volunteer, although we have explained that this will involve lots of going door-to-door, which would usually put off female volunteers elsewhere. They only ask to be given districts in the inner city, because of the unstable security situation.

While talking to them about what they are supposed to do, the name 'Jessica'+ is dropped. Aseel, one of the female volunteers, tells us that this is the hospital where Jessica was held in captivity. Both main hospitals in this city were turned into command centres. One had Fedayeen in it and was bombed to the ground by the Americans, and in the other Ali Hassan Al-Majeed was holding court for a while, before he moved to another place. When the American forces came to rescue Jessica, 'Chemical Ali' was already out. The manager of the hospital and a couple of doctors were asked to get dressed in civilian clothes and get out as fast as they can. The hospital was not damaged.

We are waiting to see what the survey will turn out. Raed is even thinking of increasing the number of the team to 25, because of the high number of casualties reported. Usually they would get at least 25 per cent more than the numbers from hospitals. 1,000 deaths is really a big number in a place like Nasiriyah.

We stay for too long there talking to the team and end up late for the appointment with the Basra team.

*

+ Nineteen-year-old Private Jessica Lynch was seriously injured during an ambush in Nasiriyah on 23 March 2003. She survived because of medical attention from Iraqis. A week later, her dramatic rescue by US special forces received worldwide publicity.

Basra is beautiful. We have a bit of a problem with hotels. Because it is chockfull of foreigners and news people, all the places charge outrageous prices. We find a place where we pay 30,000 dinars for a night – compared to 3,000 dinars in Nasiriyah (foreigners pay double that price). But there is great food and an excellent ice-cream place called Kima. No, this is not a paid plug. Go ask for *ananas-azbari* and be pleasantly surprised, it has frozen bits of pineapple in it. Block those thoughts about cholera and enjoy.

Water is a bit of a problem. People in Basra have been dependent on water purified by the petrochemicals plant or people who have set up businesses to provide clean water – they call it RO water (reverse-osmosis purification). Of course you have to buy that. Now there are purification plants donated by Gulf countries, but you still have to queue to get it or go buy RO water on the street – its price has gone down after the plants started working. All this is within Basra city. Outside of Basra? Don't ask.

The Police in Basra are much luckier than the police in Baghdad: they get military protection. But what doesn't get protection is any store selling alcohol. There have been attacks on five stores that sell liquor and everybody in the store was killed. There is no way anyone is going to sell you a beer on the street in Basra. Some areas in Baghdad have seen similar attacks, but nobody panicked yet. It is only a matter of time. Al-Fartoosi in his Friday prayer *khutba* said that 'loose women', the cinemas in Sadoon Street showing immoral films (the films are as sinful as a Britney Spears video: bellies and fake kissing) and anyone selling alcohol will be given a week to clean up their act or 'other methods' will be used to stop them spreading wickedness.

In Basra we came across about a hundred graves at the edge of the road, starting where the pavement should have been. These were people killed during the early stages of the war, when it was too dangerous to bury them in a proper burial ground. The nearest empty land was used. The latest are dated 16 April. The ones that don't have a name sign are people who could not be identified. There was another makeshift graveyard near the Dyala Bridge in Baghdad. There were a couple of people buried there, near the bridge, from Basra or around it. We wrote down the names and gave them to a couple of people who were at the cemetery in

Basra to put them up in mosques. Maybe the word will get to their families.

Elsewhere in Basra the Islamic Dawa Party had long lists of names put up at the door of its headquarters. The names of Dawa Party members who were executed and killed by the Baath. You see these scenes in all cities. When the lists were put up in Karbala (not only Dawa, but the hundreds of people killed during the uprising in 1991), you saw the whole city go into the traditional three-day funeral. There were 240 names: men, women and children – families of twenty and more at a time.

The rest of the time was spent in our way-too-expensive hotel. We only go out for a short walk in al-Ashar, by the river. The war with Iran was just over when Saddam decided to commemorate his officers with a huge monumental project at al-Ashar. The thirty officers he chose got larger-than-life statues cast in bronze – all pointing towards the East: Iran. Today all thirty officers have been pulled down from their podiums. Only one remains: Adnan Khairullah, Saddam's cousin from his mother's side. He was killed by Saddam when he was getting a bit too popular with his troops as a defence minister. The rest were pulled down, cut to pieces and sold on the market for the metal.

Next morning we woke up to the sound of a British army patrol. We rushed to the Basra general hospital and met the Basra CIVIC team – all of the volunteers are medical students. By this time I am really too fazed-out by all we have seen to listen and join the discussions. Raed goes on like one of those Duracell rabbits.

When we were in Nasiriyah, someone made a joke about Saddam and the money we are using. Aseel responded: 'Ha! So now you find your voice?'

Yes, we are all finding our voices now. Suddenly everyone has an opinion. Everyone thinks he/she should be involved. Talking to all the volunteers in the cities we've been to really gives you a push. There was an article before the war, I think by Makiya, but I am not sure, saying that Iraqis after all this time have been depoliticized. You wouldn't think so after walking in the streets these days. The people we deal with are my age or younger. We are not apathetic about the politics of this country. The University of Baghdad will be a very interesting place to be in these days.

:: **salam 1:59 PM [+]** ::

Thursday, 22 May 2003

Good news: Any Iraqis reading this? Spread the word. If you have family, relatives or friends in Baghdad and their phone number starts with 555, 556 or 557, you can call them from wherever you are. Normal international call. An ingenious Iraqi communication engineer put up a dish on top of the Dawoodi exchange and set up a number of phone booths for people to make phone calls abroad. Cheaper than the Thuraya sharks. They have banners on the Dawoodi exchange building saying COMMUNICATION WITH THE OUT-SIDE WORLD POSSIBLE HERE.

The happy side-effect is that when there isn't too much traffic, the calls get directed, as usual, to your phone at home if you are on that particular exchange. He is making the southwestern district of Baghdad very happy. Anyway. If you are an Iraqi or know one, spread the word. Start dialling.

Update: the Dawoodi exchange has been linked to the exchanges in Baghdad-al-Jadeeda, Amin and Zayoona areas. These are numbers starting with 77X. I guess you should try anything within Baghdad that does not start with 541 or 542. We can't call you from home, but you can call us.

The Iraqi dinar is having the roller-coaster ride of a lifetime: 2,000 dinars for a dollar today; 950 the next; 1,350 ten hours later. And down again. There is no logical explanation, at least an explanation an ignoramus like me would get.

If you were *me* these days you would be meeting very interesting people. There was a very long talk with mark from www.boar.com, who was on a two-day trip in Iraq. I met him after he was in one of the presidential palaces looting. He had a stainless-steel teapot hidden under his T-shirt when he came into the hotel, where we were supposed to meet. Pah! Amateur *Amrikaan*! At least choose something that looks like it could be gold or something.

Don't ask how we met. Pure coincidence. We sat there for about two hours, talk-talk-talk. He was strangely gadget free. He only had a nifty digital camera and showed me the pictures he had taken inside the palace, including the obligatory picture of a bathroom. Everybody has a fixation on bathrooms. The first images they showed of one of the palaces had shots of not-so-significant bathrooms. I am sure there will be a 'Saddam's Bathrooms' special on one of the shows soon. Anyway. Great guy. Mark, not Saddam.

A day before that I sold my soul to the devil. I talked to Rory from the *Guardian*. Look, he paid for a great lunch in a place which had air-conditioning and lots of people from Foreign. It was fun talking to him, but when Raed saw me after 'the talk' he said I looked like someone had violated me. So there is a bit of guilt. But that was washed away with the cool air-conditioning. Yeah, I am cheap like that. I would sell my parents for a nice bottle of wine.

You know how much you would pay for a pizza before Attack of the Media-Types II started? 2,500 dinars – a bit more than one dollar. Do you know how much it costs now? 6,000 dinars – a little less than $6. Plus, the exchange rate is totally fucked up and the property market is getting bizarre. You can follow the trail of the foreigners by how much things cost in a certain district. Of course, Rory didn't buy me the 6,000-dinar pizza. That would have been *too cheap*. He paid an extra $3.

So the 'interim Iraqi government' got screwed. *Quelle surprise!!*

Not too hot about any of them anyway, and this way we get to blame the Americans for the screwing-up of our future. They have been involved in creating the mess we are in now. They should take responsibility for helping us clear it up. Ummm, let's put it this way, so no one gets pissed off: pretty please, with sugar on top, don't leave now and let the loony mullahs stick me on a pole and leave me in the sun to think about my 'sins'!

Postponing the handover of government to Iraqis is a 'good thing'. It gives everybody time to think and cool down. US army patrols going together with Iraqi police patrols is a very 'good thing'. Another 'good thing' is the move on militias. There are now serious talks with the PUK and KDP about the Peshmergah, and with the FIF (Free Iraqi Forces – what a pretentious name for a couple of amateurs who ended up stealing cars in Baghdad). The FIF are now saying that they have nothing to do with Chalabi's INC (yeah right, and my name is Mickey Mouse) just so that the INC doesn't get a smack on its butt.

Note to self: Really should think about doing an Iraqi cover of The Prodigy's 'Smack My Bitch Up'. I'd call it 'Smack the INC Up'. The video would have a Chalabi double swimming naked in the dollars he stole from Petra Bank.

A new political party was added to the 100 we already have and I just realized that one has disappeared. We now have something calling itself the Liberal Democratic Front, while the Iraqi Intellectuals Something-or-other just left the show after its leader, Bustam, was arrested by the Americans. He was released, but you never heard a peep from them again. Bustam is a character who has a lot of question marks floating about him like flies on shit. He probably thought he'll just pack it in before the stink got out.

Where are those *Democracy for Dummies* books I asked you to bring along?

I tell you, life these days is like watching things in a kaleidoscope: whenever you turn it, you see something interesting.

A quick update on Raed's work with CIVIC. Nasiriyah is worse than they have imagined: 1,500 casualty forms filled in less than a week. The group there has been expanded to twenty-five. The volunteers meet with all sorts of reactions. In small communities where the people have not seen anybody yet asking them how they were and if everything is OK, the volunteers are being treated like local gods and saviours. In other places they have been accused of being Wahabis. This is very bad. Being accused of being Sunni extremists in a Shia area these days is as bad for your health as a bullet in the head – if I am quoting Ice Cube in reverse, does he become Cube Ice? In other areas CIVIC teams were accused of being conspirators in the Western-Zionist plot to annihilate Islam. (OK, that was only one guy and he probably was not in possession of all his marbles.)

Raed said that this week's trip was more dispiriting than the week before. Something in the Nasiriyah electricity station exploded and this station feeds most of the southern areas, with the exception of

Basra. The grid is down between Karbala and Diwaniya. Nasiriyah does not have drinking water at all and people are drinking untreated river water – you can imagine what that will do. An hour and a half down the road is Basra, where the RO water is now more than they need, but no one is driving water tanks to Nasiriyah.

The type of 'humanitarian aid' reaching the southern governorates turns the situation into a sick comedy. Nasiriyah Hospital got twenty boxes – six of them had only shampoo in them.

Need a blood transfusion? Have shampoo, it smells nice.

Another four or five were full of past-use-date stitching thread. In Basra the trucks of 'humanitarian aid' coming from Saudi Arabia have crates of *Pepsi* in them. The pediatric ward there is running out of medicine to suppress a fever, but they *do* have *Pepsi*. If this was in a movie it would be hilarious.

CIVIC is also trying to work with Human Rights Watch⁺ and Handicap,⁺⁺ since CIVIC already has the network of young Iraqis all over, getting the help to where it is needed will be a bit more efficient.

Look, I had this long talk with a number of people about what CIVIC is doing, where the money is coming from and all. Not even Raed – who has been very enthusiastic about what Marla is trying to do and *has* done in Afghanistan with Global Exchange⁺⁺⁺ – is very sure about how Marla is going to secure the funds for the huge job they want to do. I saw her today and she said that they will be getting a grant – but from whom?

The reason why we finally decided that it is good and OK is because no other organization has shown any interest until now to check on the number of civilian casualties in this war. The US administration in Baghdad flatly refused to do that. CIVIC people (this means Marla and Raed, plus 150 Iraqi volunteers) are, for the moment at least, the only people you can go to to ask about civilian casualties – and maybe later, after the information has been gath-

----

⁺ www.hrw.org.

⁺⁺ www.handicap-international.org.

⁺⁺⁺ The San Francisco-based human rights organization: www.globalexchange.org.

ered, something more meaningful can be done with it, more than just a statistic on paper.

One tiny bit of interesting news before I end this post.

The CIA is contacting Mukhabarat agents for possible co-operation. I swear I am not making this up. Officially there is something called a blacklist – and a greylist and a pick-your-colour list – but what is happening behind the scenes is that they want to get three different groups.

The agents who were involved in work concerning the USA, they get shaken down for whatever they know and probably will be put on trial for various crimes.

The people who were involved in work concerning Russia, they are being called to interviews selectively.

And the people whose specialty was Iran, they are welcomed, asked if they would be kind enough to contact their colleagues and would they be interested in coming aboard the groovy train?

Sorry, this is just wrong. Mukhabarat? You wouldn't get your Mukhabarat ID if they didn't know you were a sick fuck who would slit his mother's throat to get up the Party ladder. Or does Bremer's[+] 'de-Baathification plan' not include the secret-service types?

So, do I have the CIA on my trail now? They would have to wait in line, behind the INC, FIF, Hawza and every other Islamist Party in Iraq.

:: salam 2:45 PM [+] ::

Friday, 23 May 2003

Poolside at Hamra Hotel – where every journalist wishes he had a room reserved. If they sit long enough there, they could just forget that there was a war going on outside the hotel fences. Jennifer Lopez squeaking out of the speakers and cool $5 beers with over-

----
[+] A career diplomat and long-time anti-terror specialist, L. Paul Bremer III took command as head of Iraq's post-war civil administration on 12 May 2003. He replaced retired US General Jay Garner, whose time as interim Iraqi administrator was marked by infighting between the US military and the State Department.

priced burgers and salads. 'Please put these ICG reports aside, I would rather work on my tan.' Stuff like that. They come in carrying cameras, sound gear or big folders with a red cross on them. Minutes later they are sipping on a beer wearing as little as they can.

Raed simply refused to get out of the water, he kept telling me that the moment I walk out of the hotel doors I will be back in Baghdad: no electricity, lines at gas stations, prices as burning hot as the weather and a life that looks as if it will never return to normal. You couldn't define 'normal' now, anyway. Have you seen how a fish flips on its sides when brought out of the water? This is how it feels in Baghdad these days. You are not even sure if what you say is going to get you a black eye.

I don't swim. I sat reading a borrowed copy of *The New Yorker*. An article about the new X-Men movie. All systems on autopilot. I really did wish something would happen that will make it impossible for me to leave. But there are things to do, people to see, life rolls on.

I was marginally involved in something that had to do with twenty-four pizzas and twice as many American soldiers. I shouldn't be telling you about this, you will most probably be hearing about it from someone else, but it was great. The faces they made when the car stopped and they were asked if they were the guys who ordered the pepperoni pizza.

It is difficult – a two-sided coin. On one side they are the US army, invader/ liberator (choose what you like), big guns, strange sounds coming out of their mouths. The other side has a person on it that in many cases is younger than I am, in a country he wouldn't put on his choice of destinations. But he has this uniform on, the big gun and those dark, dark sunglasses, which make it impossible to see his eyes. Difficult.

Hamra swimming pool is easier.

The Iraqi Central Bank should open on the 31st May. Banks should follow the day after. It was said that the first couple of days the banks will exchange the 10,000-dinar bill for dollars, in a gesture that would show that the bills are OK – hoping to stop the way they have been devalued. Your 10,000 bill is still going for 7,000 dinars – *if* you find someone who would buy it from you.

There is another strange story I have been hearing relating to the Iraqi dinar. Mainly in gas stations, because they are the places with the most income these days, after the day is over and they want to close down. A US army car will come and exchange the Iraqi dinars for US dollars at the day's exchange rate and the Iraqi dinars are burnt at the spot. I heard this story three different times.

It is not as surreal as it sounds. Saddam printed more Iraqi dinars than the system can support. Too many dinars on the market, the value goes down and the real value is distorted. If the burning is happening, then they are decreasing the amount of paper (dinars) that is on the market, creating a demand and pulling the value of the dinar up, so it is not a 'bad thing'. I don't see a reason to be as alarmed as the people who told me the stories were.

You know the expression 'armchair psychologist'? Well, I am the best 'armchair financial analyst' you'll find this side of the net.

Talking about the net, I wonder when and who will be the first to use '.iq' in their URL? It was not used by the Iraqis during the days of Saddam.

:: salam 10:41 AM [+] ::

Monday, 26 May 2003

Internet prices are getting steeper. Now we pay $8 for an hour. Capitalism! Pah!

Someone on al-Muajaha+ (before you start wondering, the 'Salam' who works for Muajaha is not me) was out in the streets a couple of days ago, asking 'Where is Saddam?' The best answer he got was from a ten-year-old kid: 'Saddam is dead. He died five years ago.'

Well, that explains the mess.

Here is the link to CIVIC. I should put it up in the links thingy on the left. Try to ignore the quote from Senator Patrick Leahy. It gets on *my* nerves, but I still think what they are doing is important.++

:: salam 11:06 AM [+] ::

+ almuajaha.com.
++ iraqvictimsfund.org.

Friday, 30 May 2003

I really need to get something out of my system.

I got an e-mail. After throwing everything and the kitchen sink at me, they ask: 'How are your parents doing? Ah yes, your parents. Salam, people are wondering.'

Actually they are doing very well, thank you. My father was invited to an informal dinner attended by Garner✦ the second week he was in Baghdad. He also met some of Bodine's aides and has met some of Bremer's aides a couple of times too. Not to mention many of your top military people south of Baghdad.

Seriously, not joking there.

Let me make a suggestion. Do not assume, not even for a second, that because you read the blog you know who I am or who my parents are. And you are definitely not entitled to be disrespectful. Not everything that goes on in this house ends up on the blog, so please go play Agatha Christie somewhere else.

My mother, a sociologist who was very happy in pursuing her career at the Ministry of Education, decided to give up that career when she had to choose between becoming a Baath Party member and quitting her job. She became a housewife. My father, a very well accomplished economist, made the same decision and decided to become a farmer instead.

You are being disrespectful to the people who have put the first copy of George Orwell's *Nineteen Eighty-four* in my hands – a heavy read for a fourteen year old with bad English. But that banned book started a process and gave me the impulse to look at the world I live in a different way.

Go fling the rubbish at someone else.

✦ Retired US General Jay Garner (an old friend of US Defence Secretary Donald Rumsfeld) was appointed to run an interim post-war administration in Iraq. As Director of the Pentagon's new Office of Reconstruction and Humanitarian Assistance for Iraq he was, in effect, de facto ruler of Iraq in the immediate post-war period, though answerable to US war commander General Tommy Franks, who had ultimate authority. Reconstruction efforts under Garner were criticized as ineffective. Water, electricity and security services remained intermittent one month after the US-led invasion of Iraq.

Have I told you that my father agreed to act as the mediator in the surrendering process between a number of Iraqi government officials and the American administration here? He is a man with sound moral judgment and people listen to his advice. People at the American administration and many of the new political parties had asked him for a consultation.

Did I tell you about the time when one of Bremer's aides asked him what the difference between a tribal sheikh and a mosque sheikh is? They send them thousands of miles to govern us here and then ask such questions.

Did I tell you about my father's unending optimism in what the Americans can achieve here if they were given time? He is so much less of a sceptic than I am. We had our shouty arguments a number of times since the appearance of the Americans on our theatre of events.

You see, there is a lot that I have not told you about – and I don't see an obligation to do so. You all hide behind your blog names and keep certain bits of your life private.

I think the things that were said in the e-mail above and on other sites were out of line. There is more.

> **It seems your writing is dedicated to proving two points, first, mini-mizing the American contribution to removing Saddam and then, proving what terrible things the US did to get rid of Saddam, so as to paint a picture that it wasn't worth it.**

As to the first. There is no way to 'minimize' the contribution of the USA in removing Saddam. The USA waged a friggin' war! How could you 'minimize' a war? I have said this before: if it weren't for the intervention of the US, Iraq would have seen Saddam followed by his sons until the end of time. But excuse me if I didn't go out and throw flowers at the incoming missiles. As for the second point, I don't think anyone has the right to throw cluster bombs in civilian areas and then refuse to clean up the mess afterwards.

Anyway.

I don't really understand why among the 26 million Iraqis I have to explain everything clearly. Are you watching the news? Can't you see the spectrum of reactions people have to the American presence in Iraq?

I was at an ORHA+ press conference the other day (got in with someone who *had* a press pass) and the guy up there on the podium said in answer to a question, that most probably the people who have had good encounters with the coalition forces were saying things are getting better and those who have had bad things happening to them were saying things are getting worse.

It is still too early to make any judgements. I don't feel that I have an obligation to say all is rosy and well.

Iraq is not the black hole it used to be and there are a bazillion journalists here doing better than I can ever do – they have a press ID and they know how to deal with stuff.

As to the question 'why are you not documenting Saddam's crimes?' Don't you see that this is not the sort of thing that should be discussed lightly in a blog like this one. And what's with 'documenting'? Me, tiny, helpless Salam, documenting things that were going on for thirty years? Sorry to blow your bubble, but all I can do is tell you what is going on in the streets and if you think journalists are doing a better job of that then maybe you should go read them. One day, like in Afghanistan, those journalists will get bored and go write about Syria or Iran. Iraq will be off your media radar. Out of sight, out of mind. Lucky you, you have that option. I have to live it.

:: salam 10:44 AM [+] ::

+ The Office of Reconstruction and Humanitarian Assistance: a 200-strong team of former US military and other government agency personnel, humanitarian workers and Iraqi experts.

Sunday, 1 June 2003

Ya Allah, have mercy on our souls. The old state-owned Internet centre in the Adil district has been taken over by anarchists and they are offering Internet access for FREE! You just need to dial up a number – no password, no special settings. Whoever heard of anyone doing *that*?

About a week ago a rumour spread that the Adil centre has put up a sat dish and will be using the set-up the Iraqi government used to have to provide the service. Uruklink.net[+] is back. The people who used to work there opened the centre four days ago. You can have an hour of Internet for as little as 2,000 dinars. Take that, you greedy sharks! The centre is very well equipped. They put together thirty of their best computers and have a very good connection. (OK, so thirty computers in a city of five million is nothing, but it is a start.) They even got military protection. The people who work there got a couple of soldiers from the nearest army check-point to take a look – the officer asked if it was OK for his men to check on their e-mails and stuff. The reaction of the first couple of guys who came in was a very amazed 'Wow!'

Yesterday they put up a piece of paper that said: WE ARE HAPPY TO ANNOUNCE THAT YOU CAN GET FREE INTERNET ACCESS BY DIALING UP THIS NUMBER. A small little paper on the notice board. The telephone network is not fully operational, certain districts don't have phones at all, but as I wrote earlier many of the exchanges that have not been destroyed or looted have been linked together. You will need to keep dialling for an hour to get thru, but it works. I tried it.

[+] www.uruklink.net.

Not a million bad things could have wiped the grin off my face when I read that little note.

Baghdad will also be getting its first GSM[+] network in about two weeks. A couple of thousand lines as a first step, mainly for NGOs and administration. I think it is going to be MCI[++] who will set this up.

Radio SAWA[+++] should be playing the Stereo MC's 'Connected' all the time.

:: salam 2:39 PM [+] ::

Tuesday, 3 June 2003

And I was wondering when will he find out and if he will be angry, because I didn't tell him. I think he isn't:

'How do I know Baghdad's famous blogger exists? He worked for me.'[*]

He uses words like 'chubby' and 'cherubic' to describe me. Ewww. And what is so wrong about saying 'thingy' a lot?

:: salam 9:22 AM [+] ::

Wednesday, 4 June 2003

Guardian column[**]

Vacancies: President needed – fluent in English, will have limited

----
[+] The GSM Association is a major player in the global wireless industry. The mobile phone operator community provides services to more than 850 million customers across 197 countries and regions around the world (71 per cent of the world's mobile market).

[++] MCI is a global communications network and a world leader in serving global businesses, government offices, and US residential customers.

[+++] Radio Sawa is a service of US International Broadcasting, operated and funded by the Broadcasting Board of Governors (BBG), an agency of the US government. One of its guiding principles is that the long-range interests of the United States are served by communicating directly in Arabic with the peoples of the Middle East by radio. Radio Sawa broadcasts 24 hours a day, seven days a week on FM frequencies throughout the Middle East.

[*] A posting on Slate entitled 'Salam Pax is Real' (2 June 2003) by Peter Maass.

[**] On 4 June, Salam Pax began writing a fortnightly column for the *Guardian*. This is the first of these columns, entitled 'Baghdad Blogger' (www.guardian.co.uk).

powers only. Generous bonuses. This appeared on the first page of the *Ahrar* newspaper. Another new weekly. Newspapers are coming out of our ears these days. There are two questions which no one can answer: how many political parties are there now in Iraq? And how many newspapers are printed weekly? Most of these papers are just two or four pages of Party propaganda, no license or hassle. Just go print. I am thinking of getting my own: *Pax News – All the Rumours, All the Time.*

On the first page of the *Ahrar* paper you will also see a picture and a column by the founder and chief editor. When the newspaper guy noticed how I was staring at the picture he said: 'Yes, it is the guy who sells *Znood-al-sit* [a popular Iraqi sweet]'. From pastry to news, wars do strange things to people.

I got five papers for 1,750 dinars – around $1.50. It felt like I was buying the famous bread of Bab-al-agha: hot, crispy and cheap. When the newspaper man saw how happy I was with my papers he asked if I would like to take one for free. Newspaper heaven! It turns out that no one is buying any copies of the paper published by the Iraqi Communist Workers' Party – he just wants to unload it on me. Look, I paid for the Hawza paper, so why not take the Commie one gratis?

Although the Ministry of Information has been broken up and around 2,000 employees given the boot, the media industry – if you can call it that – is doing very well. Besides all the papers, we now have a TV channel and radio. They are part of what our American minders have called the Iraqi Media Network. My favourite TV show on it is an old Japanese cartoon (here it is called *Adnan wa Lina*). It is about what happens after a third world war, when chaos reigns the earth. Bad choice for kids' programming if you ask me. Some cities have their own local stations and there are two Kurdish TV channels. But the BBC World Service killed in one move a favourite Iraqi pastime: searching for perfect reception. The BBC Arabic service started broadcasting on FM here and it is just not the same when you don't hear the static.

The staff of the Ministry of Information is being given $50 as a final payment these days: lots of angry shouting and pointing at al-Jazeera cameras. Other civil workers had better luck – the people at the electricity works got paid by the new salary scheme suggested by the Bremer administration (the range is from 100,000 to 500,000 dinars: $100–$500. The people at the lower end got a raise and the people at the top got the cream taken off their pie) and as if by magic the electricity workers try a bit harder and the situation gets better.

Gas is still a problem. But if you drive fifteen minutes out of Baghdad, you'll find gas station owners who would beg you to come and fill up. Down in the south of Iraq you will find Kuwaiti gasoline, but Baghdad is a mess. There is a rumour that the gas rations given to stations here are being bought up and smuggled to Iran or Turkey. Not so strange. Looted cars were being smuggled through the same route – there was, in the middle of Baghdad, a parking lot where looted cars were being auctioned to be taken to the north. It took the western media three weeks to find out about that.

But the main concern of people in all Iraqi cities is still security. You hear stories about daytime robberies in streets full of people. The newest method is to bring a kid along, get him to jump into an open window and start screaming. Four thugs will follow, accusing you of trying to run the kid over – then they kick you around a bit and take the car. All the while, bystanders will be giving you the meanest looks, you child molester, you. You'll be lucky if they don't pull out a gun.

Actually, the coalition forces are coming down hard on people they catch in possession of guns. Car searches are more frequent and if they find a firearm they will cuff you, put a sack over your head and – here comes the question: and what? We still have no laws. A couple of weeks ago it was said that they can only keep someone arrested for twenty-four hours. Now it is said that male, female and juvenile prisons have been opened. I don't want to be an alarmist and make it sound as if no one goes out on the streets. On the contrary, a lot more shops have opened. In Karada Street, where most of the electronic appliance shops are, the merchandise is displayed on the streets (14-inch TVs seem to be very popular); schools are open and exams are scheduled for July. The traffic jam at the gate of the University of Baghdad is like nothing you have seen before. The junk food places in Harthiya are open again and full of boys and girls. The streets of Baghdad are a nightmare to drive through during the day, because of the number of cars. But this all ends around 7 p.m., when it starts getting dark.

The problem is that efforts to make Baghdad more secure are being really slowed down by the latest incidents in Fallujah,✝ Heet✝✝ and Baghdad.

I heard today that one of the infantry divisions is being put back in combat mode. The military presence has been increased in the streets and soldiers don't look as calm as they did a week ago. Al-Jazeera and Arabiya show angry Iraqis who say things about the promises that America has not kept and the prosperity of which they see no sign. Iraqis are such an impatient lot. How could it be made clear to these people that if they don't cool it and show some co-operation there is no way anyone will see this prosperity? I really don't want to see this country getting caught in the occupier/ occupied downward cycle. I know it won't.

While talking to a very eloquent taxi-driver the other day, he started accusing the media of not giving a chance to someone like Al-Sistani✝✝✝ to show another, non-militant, side of Hawza. He was telling me of a Friday prayer *khutba*, in which the imam told them to co-operate with the Americans: 'They did get rid of Saddam and they should be given a chance to prove their good will.' He invited me to come and listen to the *khutba* next Friday. Maybe, maybe. My friend G. might be right after all, when he was trying to convince me that the sentence 'reasonable imams in Hawza' is not an oxymoron.

Sunday, 8 June 2003

Go read G.'s new blog:

> So after eight long hours . . . the Americans left, confiscating six anti-aircraft heavy machine-gun bullets from more than forty hous-es. The Iraqis were furiously talking of Americans searching our

---

✝ On 27 May, unknown assailants attacked a US army unit in the Iraqi city of Fallujah, killing one US soldier and injuring seven others. The attackers used rocket-propelled grenades and small arms fire against the American troops. It is thought that they fired from a mosque in the city. Two of the attackers were killed. Previously, on 30 April, eighteen Iraqis were killed when US forces opened fire during a protest against the US presence. The soldiers said they responded after coming under fire from the crowd.

✝✝ On 30 May in the western town of Heet, mobs ransacked the police station, stoned US armoured vehicles and set police cars on fire. Residents said the problems began when police allegedly assisted US troops in searching homes for weapons.

✝✝✝ A leading Shia cleric.

women, confiscating our protection weapons and stealing our poor little chickens.[+]

Go now. I am too lazy to write anything these days. It is too hot. I have no idea how all those people from Foreign can stand the heat.

:: salam 11:30 AM [+] ::

Thursday, 12 June 2003

The king is back.[++] Well, the 'pretender' is here – one of them. I think there are three hopefuls. See 'In Baghdad, Having A Good Heir Day.'[+++]

He is the first of the wannabe-royals to arrive in Baghdad. And boy, did he get an interesting reception. It was a mess fit for royalty. You would have already heard that he came in the first civilian chartered airplane, loaded with 'humanitarian aid' journalists and his bags. His first stop was the royal cemetery where he was supposed to make a speech and meet 'his' people. He got out of the car and immediately he had the traditional lamb-sacrificed-under-your-feet thingy happening to him. After that, more sheep got the sacrificial treatment, along with a couple of chickens – and the meat was being distributed to the 'poor'. There was a moment when the crowd gathering to get the meat was bigger than the crowd cheering for him. And there was, of course, the brave young man who pushed his way thru and snatched a chicken and ran off. Everybody was after him: 'Who cares what the king is saying? Follow the meat!'

Anyway in he goes and gets instantaneously mobbed by the press, it was a scene to behold. I now have a clear understanding of what a 'cluster fuck' looks like. It was hot. The mausoleum is tiny and has no windows and you had those hordes of journalists-gone-mad all wanting to have that special picture. You can see the guy (sorry, the Sharrif Ali) muttering 'What the hell am I doing here?' under his

----

[+] geeinbaghdad.blogspot.com.

[++] On 10 June Sherif Ali bin Hussein, heir to the short-lived, long-defunct Iraqi throne, landed at Baghdad International Airport after 45 years of exile in London. Tribal leaders gathered at the mausoleum at the royal cemetery to watch him pay his respects to his royal forebears.

[+++] An article by Sharon Waxman (11 June 2003) in the *Washington Post* (washingtonpost.com).

breath. Somehow Al-Arabiya got into the burial chamber with him and got a quickie interview right there, to the annoyance of the photographers. And then the Arabiya reporter ran out of the room shouting 'Where is my cameraman? Where is my cameraman?' Oooh, it was hilarious. Sharrif Ali was supposed to make a speech to the gathered honourables, sheikhs and instant-royalty types who were seated in the garden. The funny thing is that none of them saw him when he came out and stood on the podium. Cameras and reporters had him encircled. I had two people asking me if I could point him out for them.

He was sweating. It was so hot and they had him right there under the scorching sun. He had this smile pasted on his face and a tiny battery-operated fan directed at his neck, held by one of his people. Have you ever tried to look dignified while you are wearing a dark suit under a scorching sun? It doesn't work. The moment that little bead of sweat starts running down the arch of your nose I will start laughing.

After a couple of verses from the Koran and some shouts of welcome, we get to the speech. I was waiting for the moment he opens his mouth – the looks on people's faces when they realize that he speaks pretty lousy Arabic. He has this cute accent foreigners have when they speak Arabic. OK not that bad, but he sounds strange, his Arabic sounds forced.

Very uninteresting speech. He even went so low as to fish for cheers in the most obvious ways: better wages, no gasoline lines, blah blah blah. The good thing is that he didn't get the applause he was hoping for.

Next stop: press conference in a HUGE mansion by the river. More media mobs, more nonsense. There is no flame there to inspire a mouse.

We left the press conference fifteen minutes after it started. Right outside the hall, where the media was trying to get anything out of the Sharrif Ali, we saw a huge man shouting at one of his royal highness's aides. This is what he was saying: 'Look, you asked me to drive you people around and I said OK. They promised me lunch, so why are they now not letting me in?' He was talking about the banquet that they were preparing. It was a fun day, it really was.

How these guys who were not even capable of organizing a press conference will manage to run a country is anyone's guess. And I can already see how people will react to the people who will want to be called princes and princesses.

:: salam 1:01 PM [+] ::

Monday, 16 June 2003

You take a leisurely walk by the river on Abu Nawas Street, enjoying the view. You stop when you get to the part where the palaces are and take a look (before the war, you would just rush by that part). On the other side of the road you have all these nice old, colonial-style houses. Exposed brick. Very unobtrusive, everything here has the colour of sand. Then suddenly everything jars: the *New York Times* house in Baghdad. Take a look.[+]

Wasn't there a show called *Real World* on MTV – the one with five total strangers living together? They had the most awkwardly coloured houses. Now we have one in Baghdad. Is anyone interested in doing a *Real World* episode about the *New York Times* house here? You have the kooky-looking house and the strangers – all you need is a camera.

:: salam 11:23 PM [+] ::

Wednesday, 18 June 2003

Scary War Story No. 2 (No. 1 being the night when our neighbourhood was attacked with twenty shells from a tank on the Ameriyah main road):

I was trying to get a taxi at 10.30 p.m. last night (which is a stupid and dumb thing to do in the first place – curfew is still at 11.00 p.m.), so this car stops and we agree on a 2,000-dinar fare. The moment I sit in the car, he starts cursing and swearing at 'them'. Suddenly he stops in mid-sentence, turns to me and asks angrily: 'Are you a Muslim?' He has a Muslim-looking beard, is angry and I definitely don't want to start a theological discussion with him.

+ salampax.fotopages.com/?entry=445.

'Yes, *alhamdulillah*. I am a Muslim.'

'Are you working with "them"?'

Oh dear, this is not going anywhere good.

'No! Of course not. Why should I?'

Pause.

'So do you think if I hide a hand grenade under the dashboard they would be able to find it?'

Shit-shit-shit!

'Listen, I really think you should be careful. They have equipment which is able to detect these things. You really shouldn't carry a hand grenade around.'

'Aha! So you know what equipment they use?'

Fuck.

'No, no! I said they *might* have this sort of equipment.'

Just then we pass a US patrol: one Humvee and a couple of soldiers on foot. The taxi-driver slows down and looks intensely at them. They are on my side and he leans on me to look out of the window. This is the point when I start wondering whether I will die from the explosion after this crazyfuck throws the grenade or from the retaliation fire.

He decides to shout stuff and whizzes off.

I think I was in a car with a loony-suicide-fucker last night. I wanted to ask why he wanted to hide a hand grenade in his car, but I was really, really scared. He just might decide to stick the hand grenade down my throat – because it is halal+ to kill those who are agents of the infidel occupier.

What do you do when you are in a car with someone who asks you about the best place to hide a hand grenade?

Now you might say that he is part of that movement which calls itself al-Auda ('the Return') and is planning attacks here and there

----
+ Lawful.

– I wish people would stop calling them 'sporadic', but I will get to that in a moment. What makes this guy even more dangerous is that he is not part of the Baathi underground plot to re-emerge. He is one of the loonies who have taken seriously the call to jihad[+] issued by the Imam of the abu-Hanifa mosque. And these people just play so easily into the hands of the Auda. Anyway this Auda rumour needs some serious confirmation, because I haven't seen anything – banners or graffiti – that actually names them.

To get back to the 'sporadic attacks'.

Take the events in Mushaheda village: 'Nine US Soldiers Are Wounded Battling Pockets of Iraqi.'[++] A convoy goes thru the village and gets attacked. RPGs[+++] or Kalashnikovs are fired. It is night and the visibility is pretty low. As a retaliation and self-defence, you have the convoy shooting left and right down the road for the next couple of kilometres (that is, if they didn't decide to stop and go into attack-mode – see what happened in Hir).[*]

Now when you go and ask the people in the village, district or neighbourhood about the attacks, they tell you the attackers were strangers – not from the area.

Think about it for a moment. If I wanted to instigate anti-American sentiments in a neighbourhood which was until now indifferent towards the Americans, what would be the best thing to do?

I would find a way to get the Americans to do bad things in that neighbourhood. For example, shoot indiscriminately at houses and shops.

Sabaa Khalifa Makhmoud, 26, had finished cleaning his blue and white bus on the opposite side of the road from the American con-

----
[+] A holy war undertaken by Muslims against unbelievers.

[++] An article in the *New York Times* (16 June 2003) by Neela Banerjee (www.nytimes.com).

[+++] Rocket-propelled grenades.

[*] 'As US Fans Out in Iraq, Violence and Death on the Rise' (14 June 2003) by Patrick E. Tyler in the *New York Times*. On 12 June in the village of Hir, a group of Hussein loyalists fired a rocket-propelled grenade at an M1-A1 tank in a convoy of vehicles from the Seventh Armored Cavalry squadron. The soldiers returned fire and killed two Iraqis. That night, a US armoured personnel carrier returned to Hir and opened fire. A seventy-year-old farmer, three of his sons and a grandson died in the assault on the village. In the morning, according to the villagers, military officials drove into the village and apologized for the attack, claiming it was 'a mistake'.

**voy and had just stepped out of the vehicle when the soldiers began
shooting in response to the attack. One of his daughters, a toddler,
was outside with him, and he scooped her up and ran inside their
house. The shooting blasted out two windows in his bus and left a
ragged hole in one of the bus curtains.⁺**

Make them go on house-to-house searches: tie up the men and put
sacks on their heads and scare all the children.

This would tilt your American-o-meter from the 'I-don't-really-care'
position to the 'What-the-fuck-do-they-think-they-are-doing?' position.

Take a look at the attacks the last week and their aftermath. This
sort of thing repeats itself and kind of snowballs from minor grum-
bles to calls for jihad – just like what happened in the Adhamiya district near the abu-Hanifa mosque after the confrontation between
Iraqis and American soldiers ended with two dead Iraqis.

What else?

There are rumours that a couple of high-tension electricity towers
in the north have been sabotaged. Electricity has gotten worse. We
get five hours of electricity a day in my neighbourhood – it was so
much better one week ago. People start grumbling again about the
promises the Americans made and have not fulfilled.

More?

Three tank mines exploded on the streets of Baghdad. The first
exploded under a truck which was part of an army convoy. One soldier got hurt.

The other two both exploded yesterday. The first in an underpass
right in the middle of Baghdad's Tahrir Square. It exploded under
a taxi. No one was killed, but two people got injured. The second
exploded in the Ghazalia district, killing a girl and injuring her
mother. Now this second mine was laid on the street after the
American check-point left that same street and the people there are
saying that the mine was left by the Americans, which is complete
bullshit.

⁺ From Neela Banerjee's *New York Times* article.

Sorry, I am all over the place and I was never too good in formulating an argument, but I hope I am making some sense here. What I want to say is that these attacks might be sporadic and unorganized, but they do what the Baathists want to do: creating a very tough situation for the American administration to do anything good or to keep their promises or change people's sentiments. Adding more heat to a summer which is too hot already.

:: **salam 9:59 AM [+]** ::

Wednesday, 18 June 2003

Guardian column⁺

Universities: breeding grounds for discontent? Students: natural revolutionaries? Well, not in this city. I have spent the most dispiriting couple of hours at the University of Baghdad.

Look at Baghdad. The city these days is like a festival of banners and slogans. My favourite is a banner for the Iraqi Democratic Monarchy party (don't confuse with the Iraqi Constitutional Monarchy), which says in English: MONARCHY IS RELAXXATION. It sounds like an ad for laxatives. You would expect the diversity of opinions to be reflected in the university. I was expecting heated discussions and student political debates. We never had that, but now no one is stopping us from saying what we want. But what was really surprising is that once you get into the university compound in Bab-al-Muadham you see nothing – not even the standard political banners saying HAWZA WILL SAVE YOUR SOUL and THE INC LOVES YOU.

And what about the students? Well most of them just don't give a damn. I sat for an hour with ten students under a tree on the main street in the university compound and all I could get out of them was a collective 'Eh, well . . . I don't know.' And the political parties don't seem to be too interested in getting these people's attention. With the exception of one: Hawza (the Shiite organization) is going at it in a very interesting way.

At the Jadriah campus (engineering, sciences and political science) there is one single student union type of thing that has taken the

----
⁺ This is the second of Salam Pax's fortnightly columns for the *Guardian*.

place of the old Baathist student union. You go in and meet a handful of students (all male) and they tell you about their efforts to help students, to act as mediators between them and the university staff, to provide a student clinic for free. It all sounded nice and cool, until G. decided to ask them about their personal political preference. It turns out they were all Hawza people – and the clinic is also funded by Hawza.

We go over to the place where our 'free wall' used to be (this was where the Baathist student union used to put up whatever announcements they had) and the only announcements on it were from Hawza. The only student publication, which, like the student council, calls itself the 'Free Students Group', is also being published by them. Look, I have nothing against them helping out, but the way they are doing things feels like they are eliminating – very early – other choices.

I talked to one of the guys in that group who seemed not so hot on the religious aspect of his friends' work. When I asked him 'So, who do you think you would vote for?' he said that he didn't want to get into that because it would create trouble. That flipped me into super-angry mode. I decided to stand up and declare that I am a godless Commie – and if I was afraid to say that here, they shouldn't choose a name for themselves that has the word 'free' in it.

The only ray of sunlight was a group of students and professors at the Faculty of Arts who have decided to start an awareness campaign, with political debates and discussion rounds.

I talked to a couple of women who were getting the first meeting together and it sounds pretty interesting, because they had a *muhajaba*✦ who thought that you needed a religious education before understanding politics and another who was obviously more liberal. At least you have some variety here. The students at the Faculty of Arts seem to be less lethargic than the engineers. A few days earlier they had a small confrontation with the US soldiers who used to go into the campus on foot patrols. Around fifty students stood in front of them, asking them not to come into the campus with their guns, since they were already checking for weapons at the gates.

✦ A woman who wears the traditional *hijab* dress.

Generally, the universities are some of the safest places in Baghdad. Many of the girls I spoke to see the daily trip to college as their only outing during the day. Some of them used to drive their own cars to college – now they don't. One of the engineering students actually told me that she has changed the way she dresses, because she has been approached by a student who wanted to talk to her about her clothes. He asked her if she wasn't afraid of 'the Americans'. She told him that she didn't know what he was talking about, but the next day she wore a longer skirt and said she is not going to wear trousers, because she doesn't want another one of these weirdos telling her what she should wear and who to be afraid of.

Thursday, 26 June 2003

Actually we have been having pretty bad days. If you had talked to me a week ago, I would have told you that I am very optimistic – maybe not optimistic, but at least had hope. Now I can only think of two things.

One of them was something my mother said while watching the news. It was something about the latest attacks on the 'coalition forces' and their retaliation. She said that she has always wondered how people in Beirut and Jerusalem could have led any sort of lives, when their cities were practically military zones. She said she now knows how it feels to live in a city where the sight of a tank and military check-points asking you to get out of your car and look thru your bag becomes 'normal'. When you turn on the TV and just hope that you don't see more pictures of people shooting at each other.

The other thing was something a foreign acquaintance has said after spending some time in the city on a really hot day. He came in, threw his hat on the floor and said loudly: 'I want to inform my Iraqi friends that their country is doomed.' I have no idea what that was about, but the sentence just stuck to my mind.

The last couple of days have been so eventful and I wish I have posted things daily, because now I don't know where to start. Let's go a couple of days back. Just before the Bremer administration decided that it could not delay the issue of the laid-off military one more day.

The protest in front of CPA[+]: 'US Troops Kill 2 Iraqis During Protest.'[++]

It was a bad day to start with and things have gotten out of hand very fast. At around nine the crowd outside ~~Saddam's~~ (ooops!) Bremer's Palace (isn't it funny how power drifts to the same places?). If you had driven towards the palace entrance that morning in a car that looked like it could be media people in it, you would have people mobbing your car and hitting your wind-shields with shoes. The reaction towards media that day was generally very bad.

> **AP[+++] photographer, Victor Caivano, said the demonstrators threw stones at the soldiers and at reporters, who were forced to retreat.[*]**

An Iraqi cameraman working for Reuters (if I am not mistaken) was hit badly on the head and had to be rescued by the American soldiers. And it kept getting more and more heated. When I got there the bullets were already shot and the blood was on a couple of demonstrators' shirts, but the big mass had broken up. Most of them left after a couple of warning shots were fired in the air as a small convoy was approaching – and here is where it all went wrong. Stones were being thrown at the journalists and US army and someone in that convoy made the decision to point the gun towards the crowd, not above it. Four shots were fired, two of them wounding two Iraqis fatally (they were taken in by the American army at the gate and both of them died inside) and two more people were injured. One Iraqi was arrested.

I really do believe that the decision to shoot was wrong. They have fired warning shots, so why the decision to shoot and kill? They had a very angry crowd, which became even angrier after the shooting. Doesn't say much about the American ability to deal with or control crowds. Bremer, having realized that the situation of the jobless military people is getting to a critical point (you don't want military

---

[+] The Coalition Provisional Authority. The CPA's stated mission is to assist the Iraqi people in rebuilding Iraq. See cpa-iraq.org.

[++] An article on the ABC News website (abcnews.go.com). US troops opened fire during stone-throwing demonstrations in Baghdad, killing two protesters.

[+++] Associated Press.

[*] 'US Troops Wound 2 Iraqis During Protest' (18 June 2003) by Arthur Max (www.guardian.co.uk).

trained people deciding that you are the enemy), has decided to start paying them salaries and to start a small military, something like 40,000 soldiers. Which is fine with me. Who wants military? Let's just have a couple of them in cute uniforms parading on Liberation Day.

From that incident and until today, things have been moving in a downward spiral. The 'coalition forces' don't feel safe and we don't feel safe either. You can see the distrust in their eyes and the way they hold these big guns towards you when you move close to a check-point. And if you ever drive beside a convoy, don't look out of your window – they point their guns at you: aimed right between your eyes.

Some areas are better than others. You still see US soldiers in certain districts looking very relaxed, walking around and talking to people. Kids on their tanks or buying roasted chicken from a restaurant. They are on their edgier side when moving or at check-points. I don't blame them. I would hate to be in the situation they are in. I had hoped that the day when they would be moving around Baghdad in civilian clothes and browsing thru our markets, mixing with people, was closer than it looks now.

I had the chance to go to a couple of bases and talk to people there. The most fun I had was at one in the south of Baghdad where, to my surprise, a soldier came towards me with a *Coke* in his hand and said 'Shlonak?' ('How are you?' in Iraqi dialect). It turns out he was born in Iraq and left for the US around 1985. This is his first time in Baghdad since then. It was great talking to him. He came with the army, as a translator. He told me about the really bad days in Samawah, and how he isn't really sure he is glad he came back. He didn't exactly have a very warm welcome – especially the last couple of weeks, during the weapons searches.

Do you remember the guy G. was telling you about, the translator? It was the same guy! I didn't know that until I told G. where I met him. He's really a great guy, so talkative and fun. It is a shame that some Iraqis made him feel unwelcome because he was helping the 'infidel invader'.

:: salam 1:42 AM [+] ::

The most insane city. I just can't imagine a city where so much explosive metal is lying around. The latest in the line of stories which at the moment could only happen in Baghdad is an explosion on Karadah Street, just off the main road.

A photographer walks down that road and sees someone lying on the street with loads of blood around him and missing one leg. No one wants to get near him. The guy had a hand grenade in his pocket, the idiot. And somehow the detonator goes off – boom! – bye-bye leg. The funny thing was that there were some people around the guy who looked around very nervously.

No one would tell you what was going on. Until you meet the friendly small-shop owner who knows everybody. He says the actual explosion happened in a tea-shop down the road, where lots of no-good types meet. And the guy's hand grenade blew up in that tea-shop, but his 'friends' were so anxious that no one comes in that tea-shop and snoops around and finds God knows what, they clean the place up real fast, drag him to the other end of the street and leave him there.

Why would he have a hand grenade in his pocket? Well, many reasons. I don't think he is the Fedayeen type, like that taxi-driver I met a couple of days ago. It just happens to be the weapon of choice for house robberies – you can't say no to a man with a hand grenade, can you?

:: salam 6:56 AM [+] ::

Saturday, 28 June 2003

Will be gone to Basra for a couple of days. No blogging.
No e-mailing.

In the meantime, go take a look at G.'s photolog.[+]

:: salam 8:36 AM [+] ::

+ geeinbaghdad.fotopages.com.

Acknowledgements and Blogroll

My gratitude goes to the blogging community. Your support and encouragement all the way thru has been wonderful. Thanks to everyone who has read, linked or offered support. 'Diana Moon' you're a rock-star, thank you.

Raed and Ghaith, I am the luckiest man alive to have you as friends. My father and mother, I am forever grateful to you for helping me open closed doors.

The Blogroll

(Read them. They are like Frozen Yoghurt: 'it adds years to our life'.)

Diana Moon at [Letter From Gotham]
   gotham.madhoo.com/

The Legendary Monkey at [Sudden Nothing]
   vaspider.surreally.net/suddennothing/

Peter at [The Pandavox]
   pandavox.blogspot.com/

Jim Henley at [Unqualified Offerings]
   highclearing.com/

Kashei at [Spot On]
   kashei.blogspot.com/

Kathy K. and MommaBear at [On The Third Hand]
   www.site-essential.com/

Al Barger at [The Culpepper Log]
   www.morethings.com/log/

Eve Tushnet at [evetushnet.com]
eve-tushnet.blogspot.com/

Jonjon from [The Jonjon Diaries] – unfortunately now defunct but you can still find him at [blee blo blar Blog]
www.johnkusch.com/johnkuschdotcom/blog/

Circular John at [Circular Logic]
circularlogic.blogspot.com/

Ugly Fat Kid at [The Ugly Fat Kid]
www.violentnation.com/uglyfatkid/home.html